Modern Royal Fashion: Seven royal women and their style

Deirdre Murphy and Cassie Davies-Strodder

Contents

Queen Elizabeth I, c1575. The Queen's image was carefully crafted to impress and to convey wealth, authority and power.

Introduction

Queen Victoria in her wedding dress by Franz Xavier Winterhalter, 1849. The Queen's ivory silk satin gown helped popularise the fashion for white and ivory wedding dresses.

Royal dress has fascinated observers for centuries. Painted portraits of Henry VIII, Elizabeth I, Charles I, Mary II, George III and Queen Victoria hold a special fascination for us. We love to analyse portraits that depict individuals for whom dress formed an integral part of a carefully cultivated royal image. Expensive materials, richly embroidered textiles, impressive armour and extraordinary jewels represented in royal portraiture were symbols of power and authority, personal affiliations and historical continuity. And they underlined exclusivity. Until the late 18th century, fashionable clothes were restricted to royalty and the nobility. The rich materials worn by monarchs – sumptuous silks, furs and jewels – were not attainable, and some were forbidden by law, for the majority of people.

As industrial progress revolutionised printing technologies, images and descriptions of monarchs, dressed in their finery, became more and more accessible. The clothes they wore could now be imitated, and often influenced fashions.

In more recent years, the dress of prominent members of the royal family has been scrutinised by an increasingly international public. In the 18th century, newspapers and magazines such as *The Gentleman's Magazine* described and commented on clothing worn at court. Fashion plates soon circulated in women's publications such as the *Lady's Magazine* and *La Belle Assemblée,* and by the 19th century, images of court fashion were readily available. The enormous advances in printing during the early 19th century enabled people across Europe to view images of the young Queen Victoria wearing the simple ivory silk satin dress she chose for her wedding to Prince Albert in 1840. The proliferation of these images of Queen Victoria soon meant that ivory was the colour choice for fashionable brides. Growing numbers of women accessed court fashion through women's magazines such as *The Queen,* and illustrated weekly papers such as *The Illustrated London News* and *The Graphic.* This increased publicity made royal sartorial choices more even more political than they had

been in the past. The meaning an individual conveyed through their choice of textile, their choice of garment, could be commented upon widely; the aesthetic value of an outfit for a great royal occasion could be debated ever more openly. This could also work in the reverse: a member of the royal family could show his or her support for British industry and design in an increasingly public forum.

Today, the luxury, enduring elegance and glamour of royal dress continues to attract the attention of people all over the world. There is an insatiable appetite for information, comment and for the clothes themselves – fuelled and fed by international media. No sooner does the Duchess of Cambridge appear in public than full colour, high resolution images of her outfit through television, online news sites and social media become accessible in an instant; while fashion and celebrity magazines provide intricate coverage. For those who choose to imitate her style, the purchase of the outfit is only a click away.

Dressing for the job is a challenge that some royal individuals have developed to a high art: here we have picked seven prominent royal women who understood the intricacies of royal dressing and, with the help of brilliant designers

and talented stylists, developed a unique style. Each faced a similar dilemma of how to balance personal taste and flair with unwritten 'rules' of royal dressing. We look at how they dressed in response to the changing times in which they lived; how they set trends and how each woman upheld tradition or, controversially, broke with it. This book examines surviving royal garments in the Royal Ceremonial Dress Collection based at Kensington Palace and Hampton Court Palace; items on loan to Historic Royal Palaces by kind permission of Her Majesty The Queen and Lord Linley and Lady Sarah Chatto, and royal dress in the Royal Collection, the Museum of London and the Victoria and Albert Museum. These garments, together with depictions of royal fashion in paintings and photographs showcase the best of British craftsmanship and design.

From portraits to paparazzi

Until the 20th century, painted portraits and the production and publication of copies of official images of the royal family provided the only public access to royal imagery. Charles I and his elegant court, in their lustrous, jewel-toned silk satins, were captured by Van Dyck in the mid-17th century; George III and his richly-dressed family were painted in intricate detail by Reynolds and Zoffany and hung in royal homes. It was only when engravings of these portraits were made, published and circulated by print sellers that these images could be enjoyed by a wider audience.

The mechanisation of print production spurred an exponential growth of the availability of printed matter. For the first time, on 29 November 1814, *The Times* newspaper was printed on a steam press capable of printing 1,100 sheets an hour. By the late 1850s, the newspaper was being produced on Hoe rotary machines, which printed nearly 20,000 sheets an hour. These improvements in printing technology, the creation of the Daguerrotype by Louis Daguerre in 1837 and subsequent

Left Queen Victoria by Brian Edward Duppa, 5 July 1854. The Queen was an important patron and collector of the new art of photography.

Below Princess Elizabeth makes her first broadcast, accompanied by her younger sister Princess Margaret, 12 October 1940.

advances in photography enabled a mass production of imagery that made royal portraits more accessible than ever before. Queen Victoria and Prince Albert were enthusiastic adopters of the new medium of photography, but for official images the Queen continued to commission artists such as Franz Xaver Winterhalter and later Heinrich von Angeli. These portraits were reproduced in print, and then circulated in increasing volumes.

A major transformation in press photography took place in the 1930s, when the Leica and other German cameras became smaller and less conspicuous. They could use available light, so that pictures could be taken indoors without flash and, using 35mm film rather than glass plates, they allowed many more pictures to be taken at greater speeds. Portraits of individuals became less posed, and photographs could be taken without the subject's knowledge. Informal images, illustrating members of the royal family carrying out their daily business, were now possible.

The royal family embraced this change. Although still carefully arranged, behind-the-scenes photographs now offered a very different alternative to the stiff, official portraits of princesses wearing evening gowns or monarchs swathed in ceremonial robes. Informal photographs provided a more intimate view of the royal family abroad and at home, where they wore pared-down daywear, relaxed tweeds and even sportswear. In October 1940, the newspapers published photographs of Princess Elizabeth giving her first public speech with her sister Princess Margaret. It was a radio broadcast to the children of the Commonwealth who were living away from home during the war. Such images helped to convey the idea that they were a family just like any other. The directness of the relationship between photographer and subject and the immediacy enabled by informal 'snapshots' allowed a much more personal view of the royal family. The everyday clothes they wore in these portraits attracted increasing interest among the ever-changing media.

This media interest spread globally, following the royal family as they began to travel the world. Queen Victoria had visited France, Italy and Germany, and although she ruled the enormous British Empire, she never travelled outside Europe. Her son, Albert Edward, Prince of Wales (later King Edward VII) travelled extensively in India and the Middle East. Subsequent monarchs travelled frequently but Queen Elizabeth II remains the most widely-travelled member of the royal family. During her post-coronation tour in 1953-4, The Queen and the Duke of Edinburgh visited 14 countries by steam, yacht, train, plane and car. At each stop along the way, they were received by cheering crowds, all eager for a glimpse of the golden couple. Images of the tour were published in magazines such as *Picture Post* as well as souvenir guides, which included detailed descriptions of The Queen's evening gowns and daywear. As the 1950s continued, fashion magazines featured the many outfits and accessories of the vibrant young Queen and her younger sister Princess Margaret to a fascinated audience across the world.

Public interest in royal fashion reached a peak on the marriage of Prince Charles and Lady Diana Spencer in 1981. The Princess's early style had been rather girlish and naïve but she soon began to appreciate the power of clothes and she used fashion to communicate with a global audience. Diana soon developed a style of her own that the world clamoured to see. There was a feverish appetite for news of her latest Bruce Oldfield evening gown, her latest Bellville Sassoon day dress, and her latest hairstyle. News editors soon learnt that an issue bearing the Princess's image sold more copies. But there was a dark side to the profitability of these images as the paparazzi began to capture more and more intrusive images. It was a chase that contributed, ultimately, to the tragic death of the Princess in a Paris underpass in 1997.

Now, even longer lenses and ever-present mobile phones can capture royals and celebrities in minute detail and in all sorts of situations. The Internet allows instant gratification – if we like what we see, we can buy it almost immediately. In May 2011, the Duchess of Cambridge wore a short-sleeved, camel-coloured dress by British retailer Reiss during a visit of the President and First Lady of the United States to Buckingham Palace. Within minutes of the news pictures being broadcast, the dress sold out and the company's website crashed (see page 118).

The dignified showstopper

Since the development of the popular press, members of the royal family have had to tread the thin line between fashion and tradition more carefully than ever before. While many royal women and men in recent memory have worn some very fashionable clothing, they have made their choices within the context of what is considered appropriate for the occasion. Certain individuals have pushed the boundaries. As Princess of Wales in the 1880s, the future Queen Alexandra wore striking nautical-style yachting suits for daytime occasions – outside of the traditional regatta week at Cowes on the Isle of Wight. She wore tailor-made sporting outfits, cut to perfection for her slim figure, as her continued patronage of ladies' tailor John Redfern showed. Edward VII, when Prince of Wales, also favoured sporting styles, such as the double-breasted, navy-inspired 'reefer' jacket, traditionally worn for yachting, and colourful tailored tweeds. These sartorial choices were admired by his contemporaries but provoked his parents, Queen Victoria and Prince Albert, into cautioning him on the matter. As the Queen wrote to their 'Bertie' in 1858: 'Dress is a trifling matter … But it gives also the one outward sign from which people in general can and often do judge upon the inward state of mind and feeling of a person … we do not wish to control your own tastes and fancies … but we do expect, that you will never wear anything extravagant or slang'. It is still true today that unwritten royal style 'rules' dictate choice of dress on particular public occasions. For example, The Queen continues to wear evening wear for formal daytime occasions such as the State Opening of Parliament. Other members of the royal family wear uniforms or tailored day suits for military reviews. Royal dress frequently occupies a middle ground between tradition and modernity, maintaining links with the past while exemplifying good British design. However, luxurious materials, brilliant jewellery and one-off couture designs have always set royal women apart from the mainstream. At the beginning of the 20th century, Queen Mary developed a style that was characterised by a timeless opulence. Her look remained unchanged as fashionable hemlines went up and down, hair styles were cropped and grew longer. She wore heavily-beaded evening gowns and velvet and silk day dresses in mauves and blues, sporting brimless toque hats while remaining adorned with copious jewels. She was the embodiment of Cecil Beaton's claim that, 'Since royalty by its very definition is above the crowd, it stands to reason that the fashions of Kings and Queens should be individual and unique.'

However, such extravagance was not so acceptable to a less deferential audience in later decades. Diana, Princess of Wales was particularly aware of the intense scrutiny that her wardrobe was under from a fearless press and adoring public. The late couturier Catherine Walker, who designed so many of Diana's evening gowns and day suits, navigated the Princess's need for regal but understated evening wear with tremendous skill. In her 1998 autobiography, she recalled the challenge of designing evening wear for the Princess: 'I had a sort of private brief to design a dignified showstopper. It was almost a contradiction.'

Practicalities and protocol

Organising a wardrobe for a royal tour involves the most complex set of 'rules'. Practicalities – extremes of climate, types of activities, events – plus aesthetic and symbolic considerations must be taken into account by designers and stylists. During the 1950s and 1960s, the couturier Norman Hartnell created many sumptuous evening gowns for The Queen's

royal tours. He used his mastery of intricate, glittering embroidery to produce a layered silk tulle evening gown trimmed with wattle, the national flower for Australia, during The Queen's lengthy post-coronation tour in 1953-4. Later, he designed a sculptural cream silk gown trimmed with dark green maple leaves for a state visit to Canada. For The Queen's 1957 state visit to France, he produced an embroidery *tour de force* – an ivory silk gown, embroidered with vast swathes of French wildflowers, poppies and large gold bees, the emblem of Napoleon. More recent members of the royal family have carried on this tradition, wearing clothes or accessories that incorporate national symbols to compliment the host country.

The flamboyant and fashion-conscious King George IV began the royal tradition for wearing tartan during his 1822 visit to Edinburgh – the first visit to Scotland by a reigning monarch since 1650. The King arrived amid a spectacular pageant, organised by the Scottish writer Sir Walter Scott, wearing a magnificent gold-embroidered, bright red tartan doublet and kilt, with flesh-coloured stockings to hide his legs. The artist David Wilkie chose to omit these in his official portrait, which was more flattering than the caricaturists' versions. Queen Victoria and Prince Albert's first visit to Scotland in 1842 ignited a deep enthusiasm for all things Scottish. They purchased Balmoral Castle in 1852 and filled it with tartan carpets and soft furnishings. Albert wore a kilt regularly during these visits, while Victoria wore tartan silk dresses and shawls. The eagerness with which they adopted this Scottish theme encouraged the mid-19th century tartan trend among men and women of style. Many tartan waistcoats and dresses survive in British museum collections.

Far left King George IV by Sir David Wilkie, 1829. The King promoted a royal tradition for wearing tartan and elevated the kilt to become the national dress for Scotland.

Left This satirical print of King George IV in a kilt was published after his visit to Edinburgh in 1822.

Right This evening dress by Norman Hartnell was worn by Queen Elizabeth II on a state visit to Paris in 1957. It is embroidered with French motifs including the flowers of France and large gold bees.

This tartan tradition has endured among more recent members of the royal family. The Queen has been photographed wearing a kilt on many occasions. Diana, Princess of Wales wore tartan her own way. In 1982, she was photographed at the Braemar Gathering and highland games wearing a striking red and black tartan dress by Caroline Charles with fashionable puffed sleeves and black contrasting piping. The milliner John Boyd created a black tam o'shanter-style hat for the occasion (see page 97). During a visit to Scotland in 2013, the Duchess of Cambridge chose a short coat in soft blue and grey tartan designed by Caroline Smiley for Pimlico-based label moloh. Military uniform, or tailored daywear with military-style details, has been worn by many members of the royal family for ceremonial occasions. In recent years, senior royal men have worn military uniform for almost all formal occasions, as any photograph of the royal family on the balcony of Buckingham Palace demonstrates. Royal women have also incorporated military details into their clothing. In 1856, Queen Victoria wore a red wool riding jacket trimmed with military-style embroidery at the collar and cuffs during a review of troops returning from the Crimean War. The press

reacted enthusiastically to the creation, which they considered to be a great compliment to the troops. In 1942, Cecil Beaton photographed the 16-year-old Princess Elizabeth in her new role as Colonel of the Grenadier Guards. She is seen wearing a brooch depicting the regimental badge in blue enamel and diamonds and a fashionable, military-inspired cap trimmed with the regimental badge (see page 66). The Duchess of Cambridge made headlines in the fashion press when she wore a double-breasted navy blue dress by Alexander McQueen for her first official military engagement, presenting operational medals to Irish Guards alongside the Duke of Cambridge in June 2011. These military styles have lent a formality and historical continuity to long-standing ceremonial occasions.

Above The Duke and Duchess of Cambridge attend a medal parade for the 1st Battalion Irish Guards Regiment, June 2011.

Left Queen Victoria's riding jacket (1856), trimmed with military-style embroidery.

Far left The Royal Family in front of Balmoral Castle, Scotland during their annual summer holiday, August 1972.

Perhaps the most important royal fashion 'rule' of all is to consider the practicalities. First, colour. For example, The Queen might wear a brightly-coloured coat for an event at which she will be surrounded by people wearing dark military uniforms. The resulting colour contrast allows her to stand out from the crowd, making her more visible to the many people who hope to catch a glimpse of her. During a state visit, the fabric choice might be affected by the colour of the insignia she must wear. As goes for all royal women, hemlines must be long enough to be modest even when the wearer is standing on a raised platform, and skirts in light fabrics must be weighted to prevent any embarrassing moments. Royal clothing is usually characterised by clean lines. Fussy silhouettes and unnecessary decoration can get in the way of official duties, which involve getting in and out of cars, elegantly greeting Heads of State, presenting medals to people, and more.

Above all, royal clothing has a job to do. It must look elegant, tidy and appropriate to the occasion, in front of crowds and in front of the cameras. An awareness of these unwritten rules of royal fashion has been essential for royal couturiers such as Madame Elizabeth Handley-Seymour, Norman Hartnell, Hardy Amies and Catherine Walker. These designers and many others have been careful to incorporate an acknowledgement of royal tradition into their designs.

Royal rebels

Naturally, some members of the royal family pushed the boundaries. Princess Margaret enjoyed a certain amount of freedom in her clothing choices. During the late 1940s and early 1950s, the Princess's necklines were more daring than her sister's, as demonstrated by the simple ivory silk dress by Norman Hartnell (see page 85).

Left Queen Elizabeth II reviews the Guard of Honour at the Canadian Forces Base in Winnipeg, Canada in October 1984. Her brightly-coloured coat makes her stand out against all the dark uniforms around her.

Right Princess Margaret favoured Eastern-inspired kaftans, with their loose-fitting form and elaborate embellishment, for the hot climate of Mustique, where she had a holiday home.

Below right Short day dress made for Princess Margaret by Marc Bohan for Christian Dior, c1979.

Margaret earned a reputation as the party princess – a social butterfly, usually photographed with her signature long cigarette holder and often spotted emerging from the ballroom of London's Dorchester Hotel in the early hours of the morning. In 1960, she married the handsome photographer Antony Armstrong-Jones and throughout the decade she and her circle, which included pop stars, designers and actors, were known as 'the Margaret set'. Margaret and Antony wore leather jackets while they travelled together by motorcycle. In the later sixties, the Princess wore shorter, Biba-like dresses. During the 1970s, the Princess adopted a carefree, bohemian style, wearing silk, gold-embroidered kaftans while she spent time at her holiday home on the Caribbean island of Mustique.

The Duke of Windsor was an earlier royal rebel. The Duke was a trendsetter. Even before his abdication from the throne in 1936, he was renowned for his beautiful suits, his way with colour, his Fair Isle jumpers and his hats, which he frequently wore at a jaunty angle. In his 1960 memoir, *A Family Album,* the Duke describes rebelling against the preferences of his father and grandfather in considerable detail: 'I never wore a brown or grey bowler as my father, but I did in the 1920s try and launch a dark blue one. It did not catch on.' On the subject of walking sticks, he wrote: 'My grandfather and father would not have dreamt of going out without carrying one of these elegant weapons ... I used to carry one until the late nineteen twenties. Then after a visit to America, where the cane is almost unknown, I discarded it as a bit of an impediment which was not only unnecessary but inconvenient, for it was always getting lost or worse still, tripping me up.'

The Duke was extremely particular about how he wanted his clothes (all of which were bespoke) to be made. He worked closely with his tailors and other suppliers to get all of the details just the way he wanted them. A close look at his surviving garments reveals his eye for detail: buttons in exactly the right place, linings made of unusual materials. In *A Family Album* he revealed the efforts he made to get the right cut of suit, buying the jacket at Scholte, his favourite tailor, and the trousers elsewhere. 'I never had a pair of trousers made by Scholte. I disliked his cut of them; they were made, as English trousers usually are, to be worn with braces high above the waist. So, preferring as I did to wear a belt rather than braces with trousers, in the American style, I invariably had them made by another tailor.' The Duke's and Princess Margaret's rebellious but very individual styles provided inspiration for the young fashionable people of their generation. They are still widely recognised as having been among the most stylish individuals of the 20th century.

By royal appointment

For many years, members of the royal family have promoted British industry by wearing British-made clothing. The Duchess of Cambridge has made many high-profile appearances wearing clothing by contemporary British designers such as Alexander McQueen, Issa, Erdem, Burberry and Jenny Packham. The Duchess has supplemented this designer wardrobe with garments from British high street chains, such as Reiss, L.K. Bennett and Topshop.

This focus on British design forms part of a long tradition of royal support for British clothing and textile industries. From the very beginning of her reign, Queen Victoria was careful to wear British-made silks and lace for important public events. She cast her love for French textiles and accessories aside for these occasions, enabling journalists to report 'Her Majesty's dress was of entirely British manufacture', again and again. Her son, Albert Edward, Prince of Wales (later King Edward VII) was a firm supporter of

Far left The Duke and Duchess of Windsor in Canada, 1945. The Duke was renowned for his unique style and his modern approach to fashion.

Left The Duchess of Cambridge wearing a winter coat by high street brand Reiss for the official opening of the National Football Centre in Staffordshire, October 2012.

Below The windows of Norman Hartnell's London workshop were whitewashed in 1947 to ensure the design of Princess Elizabeth's wedding dress remained a secret.

London's Savile Row, where he ordered many sharply-tailored bespoke suits. The Duke of Windsor also patronised British firms. Frederick Scholte was his preferred Savile Row tailor while Hawes & Curtis supplied shirts, each carefully embroidered with his monogram. A collection of his suits and shirts survives in the Royal Ceremonial Dress Collection. Princess Margaret, never in the public eye as much as her sister, The Queen, enjoyed the freedom to wear clothing by a combination of British and international designers. In 1951, Cecil Beaton portrayed her as a fairy-tale princess, wearing a voluminous layered silk chiffon gown by Dior.

Absolute discretion is fundamental to a good relationship between designer and royal client. Before the wedding of Princess Elizabeth and Lieutenant Philip Mountbatten in 1947, Norman Hartnell took great pains to keep the details of the wedding dress a secret. He had the windows to his Bruton Street studio whitewashed in order to prevent anyone from seeing in, and kept in touch with Buckingham Palace to ensure that adequate security was in place. Despite these efforts, public interest in the wedding dress was so intense that there were several attempted break-ins. The firm's night man was attacked one morning on his way home.

During the early 1980s, designers David and Elizabeth Emanuel described their royal client Diana, Princess of Wales with a range of pseudonyms in their appointment book to prevent her regular visits to their studio from being leaked to the press. David Sassoon of Bellville Sassoon recalls making discreet visits to the Princess's apartments at Kensington Palace for private dress fittings.

Despite the confidentiality of the details of royal custom, public awareness of royal patronage can clearly provide an enormous boost to business, a fact of which designers are not unaware. In 1879, Princess Alexandra's preferred tailor, John Redfern, advertised the firm as 'Inventors and makers of the celebrated jersey gowns worn by H.R.H. the Princess of Wales.' Certain members of the royal family have the authority to formally recognise suppliers of high-quality goods and services with the Royal Warrant. Numerous fashion houses, tailors, accessory designers and perfumers such as Norman Hartnell, Gieves & Hawkes, Cartier and Floris have received Royal Warrants over the years. Royal Warrant holders are permitted to display the royal coat of arms, 'by appointment', in their shops and on company advertising. The Warrant is not intended to be a reward that boosts business but it certainly carries a cachet and is recognised around the world as a mark of good quality. The accounts of Queen Victoria's Office of the Robes reveal the large numbers of clothing suppliers who wrote to her dressers requesting Royal Warrants – even those who had never actually supplied anything to her. They were refused.

Several members of the royal family have worn clothing from high street retailers. For example, the Reiss and Topshop dresses that the Duchess of Cambridge has worn have generated huge excitement in the press and among female fans. The Duchess is not the first member of the royal family to buy from the high street. On several occasions during the 1950s, The Queen

Left In the workrooms of the fashion designer Norman Hartnell, two professional embroiderers add embellishment to an afternoon dress, 1944.

Right The Duchess of Cambridge chose a striking red hat by Sylvia Fletcher for Lock & Co for the Diamond Jubilee Thames River Pageant, 3 June 2012.

wore some vibrant printed cotton dresses by Horrockses, well within reach of the average middle class woman. These shop-bought garments hang in royal wardrobes alongside designer outfits that together showcase British industry and craftsmanship at its very best.

The very best of British

Delicate hand-stitching, intricate embroidery, expert tailoring and the best materials define the couture and bespoke garments made for the royal family by contemporary British designers and long-established British firms. Queen Mary, who favoured the couturiers Reville and Rossiter and Madame Elizabeth Handley-Seymour, wore heavily embellished dresses in luxurious materials. During the 1932 Season, when other royal women wore simple satins, lace, chiffon and plain brocades, Queen Mary appeared in 'silver tissue scintillated with an all-over hand-embroidery of cut crystals' or 'Brilliant gold lamé draped with gold tulle, magnificently hand-embroidered with fine diamanté.'

Norman Hartnell focused heavily on embroidery, providing numerous dresses for The Queen, hand-embroidered with geometric lines, floral motifs and national symbols using traditional tambour beading techniques. Hartnell was well-known for his busy embroidery workrooms, where countless embroiderers worked at embroidery frames, embellishing silk chiffons and taffetas with gleaming metal and diamanté beads. For an important royal commission, a single dress could occupy six embroiderers for several weeks.

John Lobb Ltd has supplied footwear to several generations of the royal family. Based near St James's Palace, the firm first received the Royal Warrant from Albert Edward, Prince of Wales, and today retains Warrants from the Duke of Edinburgh and the Prince of Wales. Lobb uses traditional techniques and employs craftspeople whose expertise is developed over many years. Each pair of the firm's bespoke shoes is moulded around wooden lasts, carved specifically to match the shape of the customer's feet. The lasts are then passed to a pattern-cutter, who devises the shapes of the component pieces of the shoes. A craftsman known as a 'clicker' plots the pattern on the best quality leather, ensuring each piece is cut in leather of the appropriate weight, grain and flexibility. The shoes are then stitched, stiffened and assembled, with bespoke detailing to upper and soles as required. The tree-maker creates a bespoke shoe tree to ensure the shoes retain their shape in the future, and the firm's polisher gives the shoes a lasting shine.

The current generation of the royal family has also granted the Royal Warrant to James Lock & Co Ltd. Also in St James's Street and established in 1676, 'Lock's' is the oldest hat shop in the world. They supplied riding hats to Queen Victoria and her mother, the Duchess of Kent during the 1830s, and the company has continued to make hand-blocked women's and men's hats, including traditional

panamas, bowlers, top hats and tweed caps, in a varied range of shapes and materials.

Hand & Lock in London's Fitzrovia has hand-embroidered glittering gowns for many female members of the royal family. The company has worked with couturiers such as Christian Dior, Norman Hartnell and Hardy Amies. Queen Elizabeth The Queen Mother, Queen Elizabeth II and Diana, Princess of Wales have worn dresses embroidered by the firm. Their fine and detailed work, incorporating traditional embroidery techniques and intricate beadwork, has distinguished the clothes of many royal women from their contemporaries.

Since the late 18th century, London's Savile Row has been known for its many tailoring firms. In the 19th and early 20th centuries, royal women had their riding jackets made by firms such as Hunter, while the men have patronised firms such as Dege & Skinner, Henry Poole & Co, Gieves & Hawkes, Frederick Scholte and Davies & Son. Although Savile Row has changed in many ways over the years, it remains the best place in the world to buy a bespoke suit. Royal patronage of Savile Row, as well as Lobb, Lock's, Hand & Lock and many other British makers, has helped to ensure that the detailed knowledge and skill held by hundreds of knowledgeable and talented craftspeople will be passed from the current generation into the future.

Left Royal couturier Hardy Amies and his team leave Savile Row for Clarence House, to deliver clothes for Princess Elizabeth's upcoming Australian tour, January 1952.

Right Diana, Princess of Wales wearing one of Catherine Walker's 'dignified showstoppers' at the London Coliseum, July 1989.

....

For all the traditional aspects of royal fashion, members of the royal family have also looked to the future when choosing how to dress. Fashionable individuals such as Princess Alexandra, Diana, Princess of Wales and Princess Margaret have helped to launch the careers of previously unknown designers and makers. For example, Diana's decision to commission a wedding dress from David and Elizabeth Emanuel sent the pair's business soaring just shortly after they graduated from the Royal College of Art. Royal rebels such as the Duke of Windsor have continually bent the unwritten royal fashion rules, gaining fashion followers all over the world. Since the beginning of the 20th century, royal fashion has represented the best of British craft and design. Designers such as Catherine Walker have consistently found clever ways to operate within the 'rules' of royal dressing. The sleek, unfussy silhouettes she designed for the Princess of Wales adhered to necessary etiquette while helping to modernise the Princess's public image. This creative tension between tradition and modernity continues to make royal fashion alluring to a global audience. Dramatic changes in image-making and communication have made royal fashion more accessible than ever. Through new media channels, the new generation's interpretation of the royal fashion 'rules' will help to preserve the skills of traditional British makers and promote good British design across the world.

Queen Alexandra

'Tall and graceful, and invariably dressed in what appears just the right thing for the occasion ... Every detail of her costume seems to have been made for her and her alone. She has an artistic sense of the fitness of things.'

1844–1925
Born Princess Alexandra of Denmark, 1 December 1844
Married Albert Edward, Prince of Wales (later King Edward VII), 10 March 1863
Coronation 9 August 1902 (Queen Consort)
Died 20 November 1925

Princess Alexandra of Denmark held the title Princess of Wales for the longest period in royal history. Her marriage to Albert Edward, Prince of Wales was arranged by Edward's mother, Queen Victoria, who then reigned for another 39 years. In 1902, the Prince and Princess were crowned King Edward VII and Queen Alexandra.

The young, slender Danish woman Alexandra brought some glamour to the monarchy. Queen Victoria had dressed in black since the death of her beloved husband, Prince Albert, in 1861, and in her deepest mourning had retreated from public duty. Alexandra was young, beautiful, sweet-natured and had unique fashion sense – the opposite to the mournful Queen. Although under the watchful eye of the Queen, who believed that too much attention on fashion was frivolous and improper, Alexandra had an independent spirit and created her own identity. She was obliged to dress in mourning clothes as a member of the Queen's court, but with her innate fashion sense she managed to be both respectful and stylish. For her arrival in England she was dressed in appropriate half-mourning purples, made from rich Irish poplins and luxurious velvets.

As Princess of Wales, Alexandra was described by one biographer as 'Tall and graceful, and invariably dressed in what appears just the right thing for the occasion ... Every detail of her costume seems to have been made for her and her alone. She has an artistic sense of the fitness of things.' Dressmakers were naturally desperate to clothe her, as her patronage guaranteed custom from her many admirers and imitators. One of the leading Parisian couturiers of the time, Charles Frederick Worth, even created a style of dress in her name: 'The Princess Line'. She later purchased dresses from him.

Left Princess Alexandra at Cowes in 1884 wearing a navy-inspired outfit. Sporting clothes such as this yachting dress, possibly made by tailors Redfern & Sons, reflected Princess Alexandra's bold and playful approach to dressing. Photographs of the Princess wearing these nautical-style garments sparked a craze for sailor-styles for both men and women during the second half of the 19th century.

The wide availability of images of Princess Alexandra meant her fashion choices and style could be copied by society women, and she set a number of trends. Alexandra favoured large beaded chokers and high necklines, which hid a small scar on her neck. This look was widely imitated at court. When an illness left the Princess with a limp, it became de rigeur in fashionable circles to walk in a similar way.

Alexandra's frequent trips to Cowes, for the Isle of Wight regatta with the Prince of Wales, inspired a playful, nautical look that became fashionable in the 1860s and 1870s. This soon developed into a widespread fashion for tailored sporting clothes for women. Men's tailors, such as Redfern & Sons of Curzon Street in Mayfair, branched out into women's wear, making tailored outfits for sailing, golfing, riding and shooting. By 1888 Redfern & Sons had received the Royal Warrant, a sign of royal recognition of the high standard of goods it produced. As Royal Warrant holders, the tailors were permitted to identify their royal patronage on their dress labels, which included the royal coat of arms and read 'By special appointment to Her Majesty the Queen and HRH the Princess of Wales.' This royal seal of approval no doubt helped Redfern to become so successful that the company was able to open a branch in Paris. Unusually, for a period when French fashion was so dominant, London led the way in women's tailored costumes. Princess Alexandra also bought tailored clothing from Gent and Son of Birmingham and Albert Phillips and John Morgan and Son at Cowes on the Isle of Wight.

Princess Alexandra remained decidedly European and certainly had a cosmopolitan approach to fashion. In the 19th and early 20th centuries, Paris was the undisputed fashion capital of the world and the self-consciously fashionable Alexandra gravitated towards French designers. During her first visit to Paris as Queen Consort in 1907, Lord Esher, one of the King's advisers, noted that she 'walked about the Rue de la Paix with Lady Gosford, and delighted in all the shops. She thought everything very cheap, and bought up half the town. At the "receptions" she was at her very best … The Parisians had never seen anything like her.'

Five years earlier, the coronation of King Edward VII and Queen Alexandra in August 1902 had ushered in a new, modern and fashionable monarchy; a new century and an age defined by wealth and decadence. The social whirl of balls and parties demanded lavish clothing with luxurious and exotic fabrics and trimmings. The fashionable Queen Alexandra was an ambassador for this new age. She was extremely popular with the public, and as king and queen, Edward and Alexandra impressed the crowds with their modern image.

Right Princess Alexandra at Cowes Regatta in 1876, wearing an outfit based on men's tailored garments and a variation of a man's bowler hat. By this time masculine styles were popular for women attending sporting events. Here, Princess Alexandra's jaunty hat and decorative details help to project an image of relaxed femininity. The jacket's smooth line accentuates her tiny waist.

RUSSELL & SONS   EAST ST. CHICHESTER

PHOTOGRAPHERS TO THE   ROYAL FAMILY

Left Detail of a dress worn by Queen Alexandra in 1910 following the death of King Edward VII. According to convention, in the early 19th century, widows mourned their husbands for 18 months to two years by wearing black. As mourning progressed, the colours of the cloth lightened and in the period of 'half-mourning' muted mauves, grey and white were reintroduced into the wardrobe, heralding an eventual return to colour.

Below Label from a dress made by Madame Leonie Duboc for Princess Alexandra in 1898. The little-known dressmaker Madame Duboc also supplied Alexandra's youngest daughter Maud, who became Queen of Norway in 1905. Princess Alexandra purchased clothing from a wide variety of suppliers including Doucet, Charles Frederick Worth, and the tailoring firm Redfern & Sons.

Right Queen Alexandra retained her youthful, glamorous appearance into her later years. This photograph by Vandyk was taken in 1921 when she was in her mid-seventies.

A 'rustic goddess'

Far right Albert Edward, Prince of Wales and Alexandra, Princess of Wales, on their wedding day, 10 March 1863. Queen Victoria insisted on having a say in what her future daughter-in-law wore on her wedding day. Victoria's doting uncle, King Leopold of Belgium, sent an exquisite dress of Brussels lace as a gift to the bride, but the Queen had other ideas. She had the dress sent back, declaring that Alexandra must wear a British-made gown, just as she had done in 1840. A dress of English silk was made for the young bride, and it was lavishly trimmed with Honiton lace from Devon and patterned with roses, shamrocks and thistles – the floral emblems of the United Kingdom.

Above Alexandra, Princess of Wales by William Powell Frith, 1867. When the Prince of Wales saw his bride, he likened her to a 'rustic goddess'.

Left Queen Victoria, who was still in deep mourning following the death of Prince Albert in 1861, declared a hiatus in mourning attire for the wedding, allowing non-mourning dress to be worn. However, the grieving Queen persisted in wearing heavy black. She also insisted that the newlyweds pose with her next to William Theed's marble bust of her late husband for this sombre wedding portrait.

'Alexandramania'

Left From the moment of her arrival in Britain, the press and public took a liking to the young Princess of Wales. 'Alexandramania' swept the country. The new medium of photography meant that, for the first time, images of the young and beautiful bride-to-be were available in shops before she even set foot in the country. The clothes she wore in these photographs and for formal portraits were undoubtedly chosen for their visual impact and were often designed with high contrast, graphic designs and with contrasting textures. When photographed with her sister Dagmar (the Empress of Russia) she enjoyed the visual humour of dressing in identical or near identical clothing, which emphasised how similar they looked to one another.

Above right Alexandra's fiercely individual style even extended to her shoes. These beautiful, bespoke handmade boots are of dark purple glacé kid leather, which gives them an almost metallic shine. Although these would have been barely visible under her long skirts, they remain a fashion statement in themselves.

Right Wide beaded chokers and high necklines were a staple for Alexandra because they hid a small scar on her neck. This bodice of silk taffeta and lace has a high collar formed from a separate shaped piece of lace. The bodice is covered in fine cotton, Brussels (not British) lace patterned with large floral motifs. The silk has lost its colour but was originally mauve, creating a striking contrast between the lace and the under layer, which would have made the pattern more visible.

A certain 'je ne sais quoi'

Far right This bodice is part of a dress worn at the christening of Queen Alexandra's nephew, Prince Edward of York (later King Edward VIII), in 1894. The dress was created by French couturier Madame Fromont of the Rue de la Paix, Paris. It was extremely fashionable, with large 'leg of mutton' sleeves and high collar. The elaborate design combines five different fabrics. The sleeves are cut in purple (faded to grey) silk satin with small black polka dots. The front of the bodice is formed of a panel of ivory silk satin covered in needle lace with a bold floral motif. The collar, waist and cuffs are trimmed with black silk moiré.

Below left Detail of the bodice, shown opposite. Princess Alexandra's European heritage may be the reason why she focussed less on promoting home industries than other members of the royal family such as Queen Victoria, who wore clothing of British manufacture for all public events. The bold combination of materials gives this Paris-made dress a distinctly continental feel.

Below Princess Alexandra wearing the dress shown opposite at the christening of Prince Edward of York in 1894. Also shown are Queen Victoria and the Prince's mother, Victoria Mary, Duchess of York (later Queen Mary).

'I shall wear exactly what I like'

After the death of Queen Victoria in 1901, Alexandra declared 'Now I shall do as I like.' The first expression of this came with choosing her dress for the coronation ceremony when she stated to her advisers, 'I know better than all the milliners and antiquaries. I shall wear exactly what I like and so shall my ladies!' Her choice was a characteristically cosmopolitan creation.

The fabric for her coronation dress, a shimmering gold tissue overlaid with tulle, embroidered with gold and silver flowers and sparkling spangles, was woven in India and made into a bodice and skirt by Parisian dressmaker 'Thorin-Blossier'. The dress was highly fashionable in shape, fitted close in the bodice with a low neckline and pointed waist leading to a flared, gored skirt. A standing collar framed the extravagant display of jewels and pearls around her neck. The one British-made item was her long court train made by Marshall and Snelgrove, but even this was in a dramatic petunia purple rather than the traditional violet shot with crimson.

Left King Edward VII and Queen Alexandra's coronation was the first to be photographed. Although the images of Alexandra's dress were black and white, the luxurious materials of her gown and robe were captured clearly.

Above Queen Alexandra's Crown, 1902. The design of this elegant coronation crown broke with tradition and was made with eight half arches in the continental style, rather than the standard four arches of British crowns. It was set with the famous Koh-i-Noor diamond for the coronation. The crown is now on display at the Tower of London.

Queen Mary in c1935.
This dove grey coat with
fur trim and matching
hat is typical of Queen
Mary's daytime style.
Fine materials and a
subdued colour palette
helped to create a look
that sat quite apart
from current fashions.

Queen Mary

'There is no one who can give an effect such as she.' Cecil Beaton

1867–1953
Born Princess Mary of Teck, 26 May 1867
Married Prince George, Duke of York (later King George V), 6 July 1893
Coronation 22 June 1911 (Queen Consort)
Died 24 March 1953

When Princess Mary ('May') of Teck married Prince George in 1893 she surrendered her personal style to the greater task of dressing for her royal role. Her husband, who later became King George V had acquired none of his father, King Edward VII's, love of fashionable dress. Instead, he adopted more closely his grandmother Queen Victoria's attitudes to changing fashions. His wardrobe contained many uniforms and he patronised the same tailors for the same styles throughout his life. Likewise, Queen Mary maintained a consistent look throughout her life. By and large, her style remained unchanged from their coronation in 1911 until her death in 1953.

This timeless quality, combined with a statuesque figure, made the Queen an imposing character. MP Henry 'Chips' Channon described meeting Queen Mary as 'like talking to St Paul's Cathedral'. She was seen as stoic and regal, quite set apart from popular changing fashions. Within her consistent style there were variations in dress for daywear and evening. During the day, tailored garments of greys, mauves, rose pinks, beiges and delphinium blues were worn, paired with low-heeled buttoned shoes and tall, crown-like toques worn high on her head. Like her wardrobe, the Queen's hairstyle stayed firmly fixed. In the evening, stately gowns of the same colour-palette, heavily-beaded and embroidered with metallic threads were worn with copious jewels. By the 1930s, the Queen's evening gowns followed a near identical cut, varying only slightly in their material and decoration. This very grand, unique style sat quite apart from the fashion of the day but the consistency of Queen Mary's look provided a reassuring constant throughout a period of much change for the royal family and for society as a whole. During the Second World War, the writer Osbert Sitwell said she had 'the particular film-star glamour that in advanced age overtook her appearance, and made her, with the stylisation of her clothes, such an attractive as well as imposing figure'.

A series of diaries in the Royal Archives reveal Queen Mary's clothing choices in the period from 1911 to 1941. In six small, leather-bound books, her dressers recorded details of her outfits and accessories, the name of their designers and the occasions on which they were worn. These diaries show how, in contrast to Queen Alexandra's cosmopolitan approach to dressing, Queen Mary made a point of wearing British-made clothes. Madame Elizabeth Handley-Seymour and Reville Ltd of Hanover Square, London supplied much of her wardrobe.

Reville Ltd began life as Reville and Rossiter in 1903, founded by William Wallace Terry and Sarah Rossiter, who were appointed court dressmakers to Queen Mary in 1910. They made her coronation gown in 1911, and supplied the Queen with variations on that theme from then on. The evening dresses they designed for her were incredibly lavish – several featured a layer of heavily-beaded fine silk chiffon over gold or silver lamé. Photographs of the Queen and newspaper reports of the garments she wore at public events reveal her highly decorative style. In 1914, *The Times* recorded her appearance at a state ball at Buckingham Palace, wearing 'a gown of grey and silver broche with corsage of silver embroidery and diamanté, crown of diamonds with the lesser stars of Africa, the Koh-i-noor, with diamond bows arranged as Stomacher, necklace and collar of diamonds, the Order of the Garter'.

Norman Hartnell began designing for Queen Mary during the late 1930s. In his autobiography *Silver and Gold,* he described submitting sketches to Marlborough House for the Queen's approval. He noted his uncertainty about how to represent her distinctive likeness in his illustrations. After some deliberation, he settled on a 'medium likeness' – a representation that looked neither too much like her, nor too un-royal. The last dress Hartnell designed for the Queen was a dress and coat of gold tissue embossed with dark turquoise cut velvet for the wedding of her granddaughter Princess Elizabeth to Lieutenant Philip Mountbatten in 1947.

Above Queen Mary with her granddaughters, Princesses Elizabeth and Margaret, during a tour of London Docks, 1938. A small number of designers, including Reville and Madame Elizabeth Handley-Seymour, created a personal style for Queen Mary that she retained for the rest of her life.

Right Queen Mary by Lafayette, 1923. Court presentation ceremonies at Buckingham Palace were formal but glamorous events. Here, Queen Mary is pictured wearing her court dress, for the second court of the Season.

'Very simply and prettily dressed'

Left Prince George, Duke of York and Princess Mary of Teck on their wedding day, 6 July 1893. Prince George wears naval uniform with the Collar of the Order of the Garter.

Right Princess Mary's wedding gown was made of ivory silk satin woven in Spitalfields, East London and brocaded with ivory and silver thread in a floral motif incorporating the national symbols of roses, shamrocks and thistles. The tightly-fitted bodice and wide skirt were trimmed with Honiton lace and orange blossom. With the exception of the lace veil, worn by Mary's mother at her own wedding in 1866, the bride's dress was entirely of British manufacture. Queen Victoria wrote: 'Dear May looked so pretty & quiet & dignified. She was vy. Simply & prettily dressed.'

Below Princess Mary's wedding shoes would have barely been visible under the long skirt of her dress. They are exquisitely made, in kid leather covered with ivory coloured silk satin, embroidered with flowers in silver thread and decorated with a small ornamental diamanté buckle. The shoes have a low concave 'Louis heel', a popular 18th-century style that was revived in the late 19th century. The inside of the shoe holds the maker's label 'Moykopf of Burlington Arcade, London', and the soles are marked by hand with the words, 'HRH Duchess of York Wedding Shoes July 6th 1893.'

'Dear May looked so pretty & quiet & dignified. She was [very] simply & prettily dressed and wore her mother's veil lace.'

Queen Victoria

Best of British

Right The clothes in Princess Mary's wedding trousseau were, like her wedding dress, all made in Britain. This tailored costume by Redfern & Sons was Mary's going-away outfit. Made of ivory corded silk it is embroidered front and back with scrolling patterns in gold thread interspersed with clusters of tiny gilt metal beads in the shape of flowers. The tight bodice, gored skirt, high neck and full leg of mutton sleeves were all features of high fashion of the early 1890s. The outfit was finished with a matching shoulder cape and a small bonnet decorated with white rosebuds and ostrich feathers.

Far right *Princess Victoria Mary of Teck, with her mother, choosing her wedding trousseau, May 1893* by Arthur Hopkins. The *Lady's Pictorial* described the 40 outdoor dresses, 15 ball gowns, five tea dresses and numerous accessories that the newlywed Princess took on her honeymoon to York Cottage on the Sandringham estate. Princess Mary remarked 'We get trousseau things sent to us on approval from all parts of England, Scotland and Ireland so that we are nearly driven mad and have not a moment's peace.'

Below The Princess's going-away shoes were by Charles Moykopf, London. Made of leather and lined with white kid, they were embroidered with gold thread.

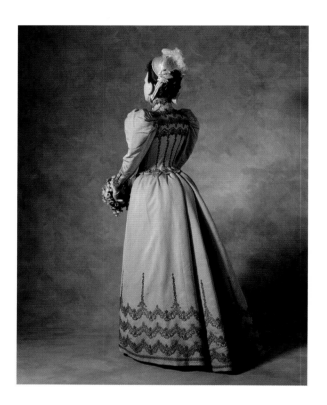

Left Although dated 1935, the shape of the Queen's Silver Jubilee gown with its tight sleeves and slight train, more closely resembles Edwardian dress from the beginning of the century. Made of silver lamé, the dress is overlaid with fine machine lace in a large floral design. The front of the dress has a shallow v-shaped décolletage with a self-coloured thin fabric insert which also forms the high neck. The dress is simple in its construction with the exception of slight ruching and a shorter over layer forming gigot sleeves. There is boning in the bodice and a slit for a pocket that is finished around the edge but not lined. This single pocket is a common feature of Queen Mary's dresses and was probably used to store her lorgnette, a pair of spectacles held up to the face with a handle.

Right The Silver Jubilee dress was worn with a matching toque of woven straw covered with silver lamé and fine embroidered tulle lace. A white osprey plume aigrette sits at the back and is decorated with twisted silver metal wires. Toques such as these defined Queen Mary's daywear look. Having settled on a consistent style of headwear and trusted milliners, it is said that Mary did not waste time with fittings. Instead, her hats were made on blocks of the correct size and sent directly to the palace.

'The all weather model'

Above King George V and Queen Mary reigned for 26 years. At their Silver Jubilee celebrations in 1935 the Queen wore an outfit typical of her style. Royal photographer Cecil Beaton attended the celebrations and noted,

'However tiresome and perverse we may be about our Queen's clothes in our more analytical moments there is no one who can give an effect such as she. Any beauty one could mention pales beside her, and to see her today was an unforgettable delight.'

'Neat, ladylike and elegant'

Far right This silver lamé evening dress embroidered with silver metal floral motifs was made for Queen Mary by Reville, *c*1934. It has a discreet pocket on the right-hand side to hold her lorgnette. In contrast, fashionable evening wear of this date was sleek, simple and slinky. Often made of plain satin fabrics, fashionable dresses were cut on the bias and exploited the curves of the female form. The Queen's tendency to choose clothing outside of mainstream fashion was noted early on by women's periodical the *Lady's Pictorial* who commented, 'Princess May cannot be called a dressy woman and has no extravagant taste in dress, preferring always to look neat, ladylike and elegant, to keeping in the forefront of fashion.'

Below left A Reville label inside one of Queen Mary's evening dresses. Reville supplied many of Queen Mary's dresses and in 1910 was appointed court dressmaker to the Queen.

Below This detail from a gold lamé dress made for the Queen by Reville in the 1930s, shows the intricate decoration on her evening dresses, many of which are almost indistinguishable from each other in style, and very difficult to date.

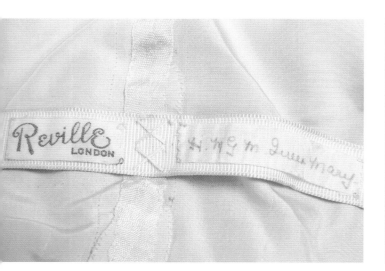

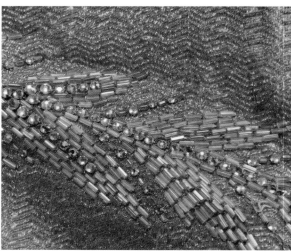

'Princess May cannot be called a dressy woman and has no extravagant taste in dress, preferring always to look neat, ladylike and elegant, to keeping in the forefront of fashion.'

Lady's Pictorial

Queen Elizabeth, The Queen Mother

'A spellbinding Queen'

1900–2002
Born Lady Elizabeth Bowes-Lyon, 4 August 1900
Married Albert, Duke of York (later King George VI), 26 April 1923
Coronation 12 May 1937 (Queen Consort)
Died 30 March 2002

Thrust into the spotlight after the abdication crisis in 1936, Queen Elizabeth's style evolved as a response to the need to restore faith in the monarchy rather than a desire to follow fashion trends. As a young bride and mother in the 1920s, Elizabeth, Duchess of York as she was then known, was a moderately fashionable but unexceptional dresser. She wore the shorter hemlines and shift-style dresses of the 1920s paired with fashionable low-brimmed cloche hats, but favoured conservative British fashion houses such as Madame Elizabeth Handley-Seymour rather than the more avant-garde French designers of the era. When she became Queen Consort in 1936 it was thought vitally important to create a distance in public consciousness between the new king and queen and the scandal surrounding the abdication of King Edward VIII. Staunchly nationalistic Elizabeth conveyed notions of tradition, femininity and family-mindedness in contrast to Edward's wife, the American divorcee Wallis Simpson, who was modern, chic and did not have children. This very British notion of a reassuring, traditional monarchy satisfied an insecure interwar public who felt increasingly suspicious of foreign influence.

The first state visit to France in 1938, the year after the coronation, presented the perfect opportunity to update the Queen's image. Norman Hartnell, whose first royal commission - a wedding dress for the future Duchess of Gloucester in 1935 - had been deemed an enormous success, was commissioned to make Queen Elizabeth's wardrobe for the trip. Hartnell designed over 30 dresses for the visit to France. With his background as a costume designer for theatre, he undertook detailed research into the 'stage' on which the dresses would be worn, carefully planning colour schemes to fit into the surroundings where the events of the tour would take place and the uniforms worn by other 'players' on the stage, such as ceremonial guards. But these subtle colour plays and designs were never seen, as just five days before they were due to leave for France the Queen's mother died and the court was plunged into mourning.

Left Queen Elizabeth photographed in the gardens of Buckingham Palace by Cecil Beaton in 1939 wearing one of the dresses from the 'White Wardrobe' created for the state visit to France in the previous year. This romantic style was to become the Queen Consort's signature look.

Recognising the importance of the trip for Anglo-French relations, the Queen agreed to leave two weeks later than planned and Hartnell was given this time to frantically re-design the entire wardrobe in mourning-appropriate colours. Not content with the gloomy palette of the traditional purples and blacks of mourning clothes for a summer trip, Hartnell, with a stroke of genius after discussion with the Queen, decided to revive the French court tradition of white mourning dress and instead designed every outfit for the visit in white. The resulting 'White Wardrobe' would go down in history as one of the greatest moments in royal dressing. The Queen left England clothed in black and stepped off the royal train in Paris dressed head to toe in white.

Queen Elizabeth continued the royal tradition of wearing British-made clothes in public. Norman Hartnell made his first visit to Buckingham Palace in 1937, when he was asked to design coronation dresses for the maids of honour to wear at Westminster Abbey. He later became the Queen's Principal Designer and was knighted in 1977 for his services to the Royal Household.

Hartnell continued to design for Queen Elizabeth according to principles he termed 'dress diplomacy'. He ensured that for each royal tour she was equipped with enough clothes for six or seven changes per day and that she wore a different dress for the most public appearances in each city. He quickly became conscious of the attention that royal designers must pay to security. Details of the gown he designed for the Queen to wear during a 1937 state visit from the King of Romania were leaked to the press. A description of the gown appeared in the newspapers – despite the fact that on the day she had decided to wear something else.

For the Queen's appearances at home, Hartnell designed understated dresses in pale colours. For her tours of bomb sites during the Second World War, he produced dresses in muted tones that conveyed 'the most comforting, encouraging and sympathetic note possible'. The Queen, dressed in exquisite clothes appropriate for the occasion, appeared with her family as a symbol of stability and continuity with the past.

....

Left Lady Elizabeth Bowes-Lyon photographed by Hay Wrightson in 1919. Sumptuous silk satin and crepe, long strings of pearls and jewelled shoes reveal her preference for tactile, high-quality materials and decorative details.

Right Sir Norman Hartnell by Paul Tanqueray, 1948. Hartnell became principal designer 'By Appointment' to Queen Elizabeth, producing the majority of her wardrobe until his death in 1979. There were constants in the Queen's wardrobe that Hartnell did not challenge. Brown and navy were never worn. A coat and dress always matched in colour and evening dresses were made in pale, neutral colours to complement colourful insignia and jewellery.

Left Queen Elizabeth with her daughter, Princess Elizabeth, 1940. The Queen favoured pretty pastel hues such as powder blue, pale purple and mauve. She dressed the young Princess Elizabeth in the same colour palette until the Princess began to develop her own style of dressing.

Above The Duchess of York, with her mother the Countess of Strathmore and Kinghorne, 1930. A fox stole, cloche hat and court shoes with ankle straps set the Duchess firmly in the Jazz Age here. The Duchess continued to favour extravagant materials and soft, feminine silhouettes for the rest of her life.

Right This dress of pale duchesse satin decorated with beaded embroidery dates from 1950 and shows the enduring 'look' Norman Hartnell created for the Queen.

'The simplest ever made for a royal wedding.' *The Times*

Far right Lady Elizabeth Bowes-Lyon married Prince Albert, Duke of York on 26 April 1923. For such a grand and well-documented occasion the bride's choice of dress was fashionably understated. Created by her favourite dressmaker Madame Elizabeth Handley-Seymour, it was modest in its design. Made from ivory silk chiffon moiré and in keeping with 1920s fashions, it is loose, almost shift-like, with a dropped waist and square neckline. The dress had two trains, one attached at the hip and the other at the shoulders. The veil was lent by Queen Mary and was worn with a simple wreath of myrtle leaves, white roses (the emblem of the County of York) and white heather, typical of society weddings of the time.

Right The linear decoration on the front of the dress, formed by silver lamé embroidered with seed pearls, white beads and silver thread, is faintly medieval in design and mirrors the square cut of the gown.

Above Although modest by today's standards it it had been the most public wedding in royal history to date. Photographs of the couple were widely published in the press and for the first time the public enjoyed film footage of the couple travelling to Westminster Abbey and on the balcony of Buckingham Palace, which was broadcast the same evening. In this photograph, the bride and groom stand between Queen Alexandra and Queen Mary (on the left) and King George V.

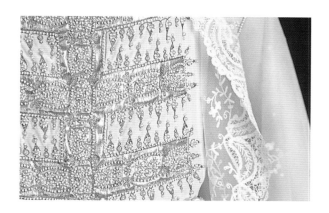

'Bright young things'

Left The Duke and Duchess of York, photographed by Vandyk in 1923. Post-war women's fashions were anything but regal in their design. The 'bright young things' of the 1920s wore their hemlines short at the knee and their waistlines low at the hips, creating a boyish, tubular silhouette that ignored feminine curves. The future Duchess of York, Elizabeth Bowes-Lyon, as a fairly conservative, country girl, did not embrace the full 'flapper' look of the era but did adopt the shapes and styles of the time.

Below The Duke and Duchess of York on their honeymoon at Polesden Lacey in Surrey, April 1923. *The Times* described Elizabeth's trousseau as 'very simple, as suits a woman of small stature': 'a navy poplin gown of simple straight design ... a beige crepe Romain frock ... which is boyishly made' and 'a plain pleated fine blue serge frock'. This simplicity, fitting for a young society woman, lacked 'wow' factor. When the Duke of York succeeded his brother King Edward VIII in 1936, a new more regal image was created for Elizabeth's role as Queen Consort.

The White Wardrobe

'Whenever I try to think of something particularly beautiful, I think always of those lovely dresses that Mr Hartnell made for your beautiful Queen when she visited Paris.' Christian Dior

Right Day dress and matching parasol worn by Queen Elizabeth to a garden party in the Bagatelle Gardens in the Bois de Boulogne, July 1938. The 'White Wardrobe' Hartnell designed for the state visit to France was lauded by the press and influenced the Paris autumn collections that year. Hartnell was awarded membership to the prestigious Académie Française for his achievements. The gowns, in stark contrast to the fashionable columnar shape of the 1930s, had wide, full-length skirts supported by crinolines and were adorned with luxurious embroidery and trimmings.

Below left King George VI and Queen Elizabeth during their state visit to France in July 1938. The Queen never wore any of the white outfits in public again but she kept most of them and they now form part of the Royal Collection.

Below right On the advice of her husband, King George VI, Hartnell sought inspiration from the paintings of the Victorian artist Franz Xaver Winterhalter, whose romantic compositions were enjoying a renaissance as part of a wider nostalgia for early Victorian aesthetics and values. In his designs for the Queen, Hartnell echoed the airy, feminine qualities of Winterhalter's women with soft fabrics and sweeping skirts of layered tulle.

'The effect she creates ... is dazzling in its effect upon her devoted but dazed beholders.' Cecil Beaton

The Fairy Queen

Left The 'White Wardrobe' created for the state visit to France was immortalised in a series of photographs that did as much to shape the Queen's image as the clothes themselves. The portraits were taken by society photographer Cecil Beaton and were, unusually, shot in the rooms and gardens of Buckingham Palace, which as a private residence, had rarely been used as a setting. The photographs were released in two batches in 1939 and 1940. Despite fears that the luxury depicted would sit at odds with wartime austerity, they proved overwhelmingly popular with the public and became symbolic of the endurance of the monarchy.

Right Cecil Beaton, seen here in a self-portrait from the 1930s, described taking this photograph (left) of Queen Elizabeth in his diary: 'Although I had no idea of the time it was in fact six o'clock in the evening – the lawns of the Palace were fitfully strewn with sunlight but the atmosphere was strange and timeless ... something like a dream.' The full-length day dress worn by the Queen is made of fine lace and silk tulle (see page 58). The matching parasol was another romantic reference to 19th-century fashion, and it had an impact on sales. Hartnell recalled that when the Queen opened it during the visit to Paris, she 'at a stroke resuscitated the art of the parasol-makers of Paris and London'.

Norman Hartnell

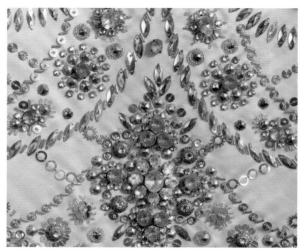

Right This Norman Hartnell dress was designed for the Queen to wear during the visit of the French Prime Minister to London in 1949 and was later worn in a series of photographs to mark the coronation of her daughter, Queen Elizabeth II, in 1953. Made of ivory duchesse satin and heavily embroidered, it features the silhouette favoured by the Queen since the 1930s, which coincided with the introduction of Dior's 'New Look'. The skirt is cut on the bias and very full, and the bodice is boned with a low neckline.

Left Queen Elizabeth photographed in 1953 by Cecil Beaton wearing the Hartnell dress shown right. The Queen was a loyal client of the house of Hartnell for over 50 years. The Queen and the designer had a close working relationship and a shared love of all that sparkled and shone. Their close working relationship meant that each new outfit required a mere two fittings.

Below left Detail of the evening dress shown right. The sumptuous embroidery of spangles, rhinestones and bugle beads forms a scallop pattern on the skirt and a dense floral motif down the front of the dress.

'I despise simplicity;
it is the negation of all
that is beautiful'
Norman Hartnell

Queen Elizabeth II on Princess Margaret's wedding day, 6 May 1960, photographed by Cecil Beaton. Beaton later recalled, 'The Queen was enormously appealing to me. Her dress was quite wonderfully romantic – with a skirt of stiff folds – and everything of kingfisher brilliance.'

Queen Elizabeth II

'The Queen was enormously appealing to me. Her dress was quite wonderfully romantic – with a skirt of stiff folds – and everything of kingfisher brilliance.' Cecil Beaton

1926–
Born Princess Elizabeth Alexandra Mary, 21 April 1926
Married Lieutenant Phillip Mountbatten, 20 November 1947
Coronation Queen Elizabeth II, 2 June 1953

Queen Elizabeth II's wardrobe has reflected the changing fashions of the 20th century – and it has been documented at every stage by an ever-expanding mass media. From very early on, Princess Elizabeth inspired imitators. Even the choice of primrose yellow for her nursery walls was widely copied. As a teenager aged 16, she appeared on parade as colonel of the Grenadier Guards in a beret-style hat of green felt that was later marketed and sold as the 'Princess Hat'. As a young woman growing up in wartime Britain, her clothes reflected the national spirit – they were practical and modest, in line with rationing restrictions. Leading designers Hardy Amies and Norman Hartnell designed fashionable wide skirts for her during the 1950s. As brighter colours and diaphanous fabrics became popular in the 1960s and 1970s these too were adopted and adapted for her working wardrobe. In later years, The Queen has developed a style that is elegant and practical for the many public events in her diary. These designs have reflected an established approach to dressing for public events: bold colours help the wearer to stand out in a crowd and suitable fabrics are selected for foreign climates and local customs.

Throughout the 1950s pictures of The Queen appeared regularly in fashion magazines and there were numerous features on how to copy her style, although the intricate embroidery on her evening gowns meant they were almost impossible to re-create. However, a Hartnell gown she wore for the Royal Command Performance in 1953 was copied by many. The full-length 'Magpie dress' as it became known, was remarkably simple for a Hartnell design: a black silk gown with a wide white silk panel at centre front. Within 24 hours, copies of the dress were available to purchase in several colour combinations. A paper dress pattern was made available for 30p, enabling almost any woman to run up a Magpie dress on her home sewing machine.

After the coronation in 1953, The Queen and the Duke of Edinburgh embarked on a five-month tour of the Commonwealth. An extraordinary number of garments were required for such a long and far-reaching trip. Although The Queen's couturiers Norman Hartnell and Hardy Amies designed most of her wardrobe, she also wore printed cotton dresses by high street brand Horrockses. The publicity helped to boost Horrockses' success during the post-war years.

Queen Elizabeth II's patronage of London couturiers Norman Hartnell and Hardy Amies helped to build the capital's reputation as a design centre for fine evening gowns and high-quality tailoring. Hartnell created two of The Queen's most iconic dresses – for her wedding and coronation – and continued to design for her until his death in 1979. Amies was granted the Royal Warrant in 1955 and was better known for the daywear he designed for the young Queen. Both designer and monarch shared a

practical approach to clothing. Amies summed up his philosophy, stating 'clothes are not to be displayed, they are to be used'. His ambition was to create comfortable, flattering garments that 'do honour to cloth'. He designed dresses for The Queen well into the 1970s and 1980s and created the gown worn for the official 1977 Silver Jubilee portrait, which he noted, was 'immortalised on a thousand biscuit tins'.

Another favoured supplier was Ian Thomas who worked as an assistant designer at Norman Hartnell from 1952 to 1969 and helped with the design of The Queen's coronation robes. Hartnell described him as his 'second skin'. When he set up his own label in 1969 he began to design for The Queen in his own right. His designs for her reveal much about the processes behind creating a royal wardrobe and the relationship between the designer and The Queen. The designs and fabric samples would be delivered to Buckingham Palace for review. They were returned with those that had met her approval marked with a tick, and any comments or changes written in pencil on the design.

As The Queen continues her long reign the diplomatic messages conveyed through her clothing have lost none of their power. The historic state visit by The Queen and the Duke of Edinburgh to the Republic of Ireland in May 2011 was the first by a reigning British monarch since 1911. It was seen as a symbolic normalisation of the British-Irish relations since the signing of the Good Friday agreement in 1998. The Queen wore a matching green dress, coat and hat ensemble by Stewart Parvin for her arrival in Ireland and a green outfit by Angela Kelly for her meeting with former IRA commander Martin McGuinness. Green, which represents the Gaelic tradition of the country on the Irish flag, has long been associated with Ireland, and The Queen wearing this colour was seen as a mark of solidarity with the Irish people. This gesture said as much about the intention of the visit as any speech.

Above left Queen Elizabeth II with Queen Salote Tupou III of Tonga and the Duke of Edinburgh, during the Commonwealth tour, 1953. The Queen wears a cotton summer dress by high street brand Horrockses. In the days before digital photography and the Internet, press hand-outs were issued when The Queen was on tour, providing a description of the clothes she was wearing and the name of the designer who made them.

Above right Queen Elizabeth II in New Delhi during the royal tour of India, January 1961, wearing a pale purple dress with matching coat and accessories. The pastel shade was no doubt a deliberate choice, enabling The Queen to stand out against the dark suits and uniforms worn by the men around her.

Far left Princess Elizabeth aged 16, photographed by Cecil Beaton in her role as Colonel of the Grenadier Guards. She wears a fashionable, military-inspired cap trimmed with the regimental badge.

Above Queen Elizabeth II inspects the Guard of Honour as she arrives at Áras an Uachtaráin, the residence of the President of Ireland, in May 2011. This was the first state visit to the Republic of Ireland by a reigning British monarch since 1911. The green colour of The Queen's oufit, created by Stewart Parvin, was a deliberate choice – to show solidarity with the people of Ireland – a gesture that underlined the intention of the visit.

Right This grey silk satin evening dress with its subtly gradated beading in an intricate fern motif was designed by Hardy Amies for The Queen in 1957 and worn at a state dinner with President Eisenhower at the White House in Washington. Amies designed for the royal family for 50 years and was awarded a knighthood in 1989 for his services to The Queen.

Above This apricot silk evening gown by Norman Hartnell typifies the new, more feminine shape of 1950s fashions, which was adopted and popularised by the young Queen and her sister. The luxurious skirt, supported by layers of tulle, is enhanced by intricate floral lace embellished with gold thread. The lace design is influenced by the traditional Carrickmacross technique that originated in Ireland in the 1820s, and is similar to the technique used on the wedding veil of the Duchess of Cambridge in 2011.

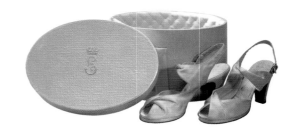

'The most beautiful dress I had so far made' Norman Hartnell

Below right A dress for Princess Elizabeth's wedding to Lieutenant Phillip Mountbatten in 1947 required a strong sartorial statement. The task of designing it was assigned to the couturier Norman Hartnell, who had long served Queen Elizabeth The Queen Mother and had created elegant evening gowns for many aristocratic women. With Second World War clothes rationing still in effect, the materials for the dress had to be purchased with ration coupons. These were donated by brides-to-be from across the country. The dress was made of silk satin woven at Lullington Castle in Kent and was a one-piece princess style. In keeping with 1940s wedding fashion it had a tailored bodice with a high neckline and long sleeves. The dramatic skirt, which was cut wide to create impact, was heavily embroidered with crystals and 10,000 seed pearls in a rambling floral design.

Far right Two thousand guests watched the bride walk down the aisle at Westminster Abbey on 20 November 1947, including royalty from home and abroad, dignitaries, politicians and 20 women from the workrooms at Norman Hartnell who had worked on the dress. The occasion was not filmed but was recorded by photographers, and broadcast live on the radio to 200 million listeners worldwide.

Above To ensure that Princess Elizabeth stood out amongst the bridesmaids and maids of honour, the young Princess wore her first pair of really high-heeled shoes, which were covered in the same silk satin as the dress, and featured a fashionable platform sole. Her short silk veil was held in place by Queen Mary's diamond fringe tiara, which was lent to the Princess by her mother as 'something borrowed'.

'A young and beautiful Queen'

Left Princess Elizabeth's coronation took place on 2 June 1953 at Westminster Abbey and Norman Hartnell was chosen to design the coronation gown. In order to achieve a cohesive look across the ceremony, Hartnell also designed the gowns worn by all the principal ladies of the royal family and the maids of honour. Nine different designs were prepared for The Queen's dress. The chosen design featured embroidered motifs of all the national emblems (as well as emblems of the Dominions of which Elizabeth had become Queen) worked in coloured silks, gold and silver thread and outlined with lines of gold bugle beads, diamanté and pearls. The expanding scalloped embroidery, which further emphasised the skirt, required a woven horsehair crinoline to support its weight. The event was expertly choreographed and Hartnell's experience in theatre design ensured that the garments looked magnificent on camera.

'Yes, the crown does get rather heavy'

Queen Elizabeth II quoted in Cecil Beaton's diaries

Above The coronation was commemorated in perhaps some of the most enduring images of The Queen. These were taken by another of her mother's 'image makers' – the photographer Cecil Beaton. In his diaries Beaton described the rush to take these pictures after the ceremony: 'The lighting wasn't very good but no time to readjust – every minute of importance. Yes, I was banging away – getting pictures in the can at a great rate, but I had only the foggiest notion of what I was doing – if taking black and white or colour. If giving the right exposure. The Queen looked very small under her robes and crown, her nose and hands rather pink – also her eyes somewhat tired. "Yes", in reply to my question, "the crown does get rather heavy". One couldn't imagine that she had been wearing it now for nearly 3 hours.'

'As a rule, ladies of
the Royal Family wear
light coloured clothes
because such colours
are more discernible
against a great crowd'

Norman Hartnell

Diplomatic dressing

Left Queen Elizabeth II is one of the most widely-travelled modern monarchs. Early in her reign she took up her role as head of the Commonwealth, with lengthy royal tours. For these trips, extensive plans are made as to what will be worn, taking into account the customs of the host country, the climate, the setting, other ceremonial dress that might be worn by the hosts and of course the occasion. There is a long-standing tradition to make subtle references to the host country in any designs. This duchesse satin evening dress, with its undulating waterfall train, was worn by The Queen on the first day of a six-week tour of Pakistan and India in 1961. Norman Hartnell cut the gown from silk in the emerald green and white of the Pakistani flag.

Above right The Queen wearing the Hartnell dress shown left at a banquet hosted by President Ayub Khan of Pakistan on 1 February 1961. The front of the gown is plain in order to display clearly The Queen's insignia. Pin marks are still visible where the ribbons and orders have been secured. The slightly narrower skirt reflects the movement towards the more fashionable, slim silhouette of the 1960s.

Above left In 1959 a tour of every Canadian province took The Queen to Nova Scotia, where this dress (detail), designed by Hardy Amies was worn. The grey silk organza is embroidered throughout with pink silk, spangles and bugle beads in a pattern that echoes mayflowers, the official floral emblem of Nova Scotia.

Adapting fashionable styles for a royal wardrobe: the 1960s and 1970s

Left Although The Queen was not setting trends in the 1960s and 1970s, key styles of the time were reflected in her clothing choices. These included shorter hemlines, bright colours and diaphanous fabrics, all within the framework of a working wardrobe. This brightly-coloured, knee-length A-line dress and coat by Norman Hartnell reflects formal styles of the late 1960s and early 1970s. Its simple, single-colour design ensured that The Queen was visible in the large crowds that gathered for the Thanksgiving Service for her Silver Wedding Anniversary at Westminster Abbey. The stiff fabric ensured that the wind would not be a problem for the outdoor elements of the ceremony, and the fur trim added warmth for the open coach ride.

Above right Queen Elizabeth II and the Duke of Edinburgh in the carriage procession through the streets of London, marking their 25th wedding anniversary in November 1972. The Queen wears the Hartnell dress and coat, shown left.

Right This evening dress of silk chiffon and beaded embroidery was designed by Ian Thomas and was worn by The Queen during a state visit to the United States in 1976, and for several formal occasions in 1977. Its striking colour and delicate fabric are typical of the greater freedom in formal dress which emerged in the 1960s and 1970s, although there have been practical adaptations made for The Queen. The linear shape of the dress, with only slight fullness in the skirt, is emphasised by the elongated sleeves that reach to the floor. The sleeves feature a discreet side opening, which enabled The Queen to shake hands with people without hindrance.

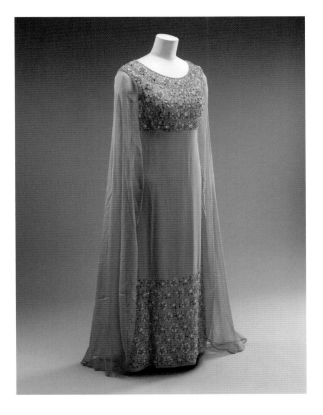

Designer and client

Below A good relationship between designer and royal patron is essential. For example, the designer must operate with the utmost discretion. If their creations are successful, royal patronage can ensure a great following and an illustrious career. This evening gown worn by The Queen for the opening of the New Zealand parliament in 1963, demonstrated Hartnell's skilled craftsmanship. It is embroidered with pearls, beads, diamanté and sequins in an intricate diamond pattern, with bugle beads forming tassel drops, alternately in silver and gold. The scissor-cut skirt creates fullness and reveals further embroidery underneath.

Right Angela Kelly has been Personal Assistant and Senior Dresser to The Queen since 2001. She has been credited with rejuvenating The Queen's wardrobe with colour blocking, superb tailoring, striking accessories and strong details. This primrose yellow ensemble worn by The Queen at the wedding of Prince William and Catherine Middleton in 2011 typifies Kelly's designs. The matching dress and coat of wool crepe is hand-embellished at the neckline with beads in a design of sun rays and is paired with a hat in a matching primrose colour.

Below The Queen, wrapped up warmly during a royal tour of Slovakia in October 2008, which included visits to a ski resort and an ice hockey stadium. Fur details add a functional yet regal touch.

Princess Margaret photographed by Cecil Beaton for her 21st birthday in 1951. From early adulthood, the Princess was at ease with being photographed and understood the importance of dressing well for the camera. She said of her clothing choices, 'I have to have things which photograph well; there's no use in having a really pretty dress which does not photograph.'

Princess Margaret

'The Princess ... rapidly established herself as a leader of fashion.
The Margaret look came to mean simple elegance for the younger set.'
Illustrated London News, 15 August 1953

1930–2002
Born Princess Margaret Rose, 21 August 1930
Married Antony Armstrong-Jones, 6 May 1960 (later becoming Earl and Countess of Snowdon)
Died 9 February 2002

In their early years, the two young Princesses, Elizabeth and Margaret, were dressed in matching clothes when they appeared in public together. Their simple, calf-length dresses paired with tailored coats and flat lace-up shoes reflected the styles that were popular among young women during the 1930s and 1940s. As they matured, their differing personalities and roles began to emerge in their wardrobes.

In 1953, the *Illustrated London News* commented: 'After her eighteenth birthday, Princess Margaret began to appear in public as a grown-up personality ... She showed poise and charm and experimented boldly with her clothes and hairstyles'. With her film star good looks and more rebellious nature, Margaret became a fashion leader in the 1950s. The end of clothes rationing in 1949 freed fashion designers from austerity measures and saw British fashions fall under the spell of the luxurious full skirts of French designer Christian Dior's 'New Look'. Launched in 1947, Dior's extravagant use of scarce fabric was initially criticised by the British Board of Trade. However, the New Look came to represent the epitome of elegance and sophistication, and while both royal sisters enthusiastically adopted this style it was Princess Margaret

who was first to wear it. She had one of her coats altered to suit the new fuller skirts and then wore her first all-out New Look-style suit, provided by Norman Hartnell, at the Silver Wedding celebrations of her parents on 26 April 1948. After this well-publicised outing, the style quickly gained widespread popularity in Britain.

Princess Margaret enjoyed fashionable clothes and was under less public pressure than her sister to patronise British designers. For her 21st birthday party in 1951, Margaret wore a voluminous Dior ball gown, a dress she later referred to as 'my favourite dress of all'. She was photographed in the dress by Cecil Beaton and appears young, glamorous and assertive (left). Although the press criticised the Princess for wearing non-British couture, she continued her loyal patronage of the Dior label (she had visited the French fashion house in Paris several times in the 1940s to order couture dresses). She wore Dior well into the 1960s and 1970s and had numerous items in her wardrobe designed by Marc Bohan, chief designer for Dior from 1961. During his time there, Bohan gained a reputation for adapting 'pop fashion' for haute couture clients, enabling the house to remain at the forefront of fashion while still producing wearable, elegant clothes.

In the 1960s British fashion and pop music took the world by storm, fuelled by a powerful youth culture with more disposable income and leisure time than ever before. At the heart of this movement was Swinging London, with quirky boutiques on Carnaby Street and the King's Road, selling fashions that broke the rules – born on the streets and in clubs rather than in couture houses.

With her marriage to photographer Antony Armstrong-Jones in 1960, the ever-fashionable Princess Margaret formed part of the chic London set and was often seen with the music and film stars of the day including The Beatles, The Rolling Stones and Mary Quant. The glamorous newlywed couple made their home at Kensington Palace, which became the venue for numerous fashionable parties. The Princess's wardrobe reflected the changing fashions as she embraced shorter hemlines, bright colours and new fabrics, whilst remaining true to her own understated style. The American musician Louis Armstrong described her as 'One hip chick'.

Princess Margaret's and Lord Snowdon's marriage came to an end after 18 years and the birth of two children, when the couple separated in July 1978. From then, Princess Margaret spent more time in the idyllic setting of her home in Mustique. In

this tropical paradise she wore eastern-inspired kaftans, a sort of effortless 'haute couture hippy', accompanied by headscarves and glamorous, oversized sunglasses.

In later life, the Princess had a distinctive style and was rarely seen without her signature sunglasses, fur coat and cigarette holder. She remarked, 'I'm always conscious of what's in fashion … I do think that grooming is terribly important. To me smartness is not only to do with clothes, but with make-up, hair, bags, jewellery, even nails, they all add up to the finished effect. They're all important.'

Above Princess Margaret meets The Beatles at the premiere of their film *Help* in July 1965.

Far left As young girls, Princess Elizabeth and Princess Margaret were often dressed in matching outfits as seen in this 1942 portrait by Cecil Beaton.

Left Princess Margaret by Dorothy Wilding, 1953. For this portrait, the Princess chose to wear the grey silk Hartnell dress, shown right. Margaret was recognised by the New York Dress Institute as the 8th best dressed woman in the world in the year this photograph was taken (first on the list was Mrs William Paley, wife of the chairman of America's Columbia Broadcasting System).

Right The Princess wore this Christian Dior gown on her 21st birthday (see page 80). It is asymmetric in its design with a single strap and diagonal drapery across the front. The nipped-in waist is emphasised with a narrow belt and the luxurious full skirt is formed of seven layers of cream silk tulle. The dress is ingeniously embroidered throughout with gold-coloured raffia and straw-covered sequins.

Left This Norman Hartnell gown was one of Princess Margaret's favourites. She wore it on several occasions in 1952 and for an official portrait by Dorothy Wilding in 1953 (opposite). The boned, fitted bodice is expertly constructed in layers of grey silk tulle with grey lace in a leaf pattern underneath. A matching bolero hides the narrow straps at the top of the bodice. Nine layers of stiffened tulle create fullness in the skirt.

'What she wears is News'

Right This glamorous party dress, with its plunging neckline and halter-neck straps marked a departure from the demure style traditionally adopted by royal women. More Hollywood glamour than royal wardrobe, its risqué nature was widely reported by the press. The dress has no maker's label but the beading is unmistakeably Norman Hartnell. It was worn by the Princess in 1951 for a film premiere in London and at a dinner in Paris where she was a guest of Prince Paul of Yugoslavia.

Left Princess Margaret and a companion at the Monsigneur Nightclub in Paris, November 1951. The Princess is wearing the evening dress, shown right. By the early 1950s the Princess frequently appeared on 'best dressed' lists and in June 1953 *Picture Post* ran an article titled 'Fashion and Princess Margaret', which declared, 'What she wears is News. It is seen by thousands of women in person, hundreds of thousands on news reels, millions who read the newspapers and magazines'.

Below Norman Hartnell's designs for royal clients were typically encrusted in beaded embroidery. This dress reflects the Princess's preference for simplicity: the lavish jewelled embellishment is reserved for a very small area at the waistline.

The royal wedding

Right The wedding of Princess Margaret and Antony Armstrong-Jones took place at Westminster Abbey on 6 May 1960. As had now become tradition for important royal events, the design of the wedding dress was entrusted to Norman Hartnell. His designs were much admired by the Princess who explained: he was 'always so good at getting the balance right'. In contrast to the wedding dress of her sister Princess Elizabeth, Margaret's gown had very little embellishment, just a small number of crystals and beaded embroidery in white. The drama was created in the voluminous skirt – a cloud of over 30 metres of plain silk organza. The dress had a jacket-style bodice with long sleeves and V-cut neckline, and an expertly-cut train at the back. The cut is ingenious: cinched in at the waist with the full skirt draped over a mass of stiffened tulle petticoats. Photograph by Cecil Beaton.

Left Princess Margaret's wedding dress was complemented by a matching long sheer veil of silk organza, with ivory trim, which helped to bring definition to the overall look. The absence of embellishment served to emphasise the magnificent Poltimore Tiara that the Princess wore on her wedding day, which gave her added height.

'Don't forget the woman'

Princess Margaret wore this slimline dress, heavily embellished with a sequined floral design, for Queen Elizabeth II's 1977 Silver Jubilee celebrations. The matching sleeveless jacket emphasises the column-like shape and is reminiscent of the collarless styles popularised by The Beatles. The dress was designed by Marc Bohan for Christian Dior. Bohan designed for other famous women including Princess Grace of Monaco, Brigitte Bardot and Jackie Kennedy. In 1963, he was quoted in *Vogue* as saying, 'N'oubliez pas la femme' (Don't forget the woman); it was the principle that underscored all his work.

'I'm always conscious of what's in fashion ... I do think that grooming is terribly important. To me smartness is not only to do with clothes, but with make-up, hair, bags, jewellery, even nails, they all add up to the finished effect. They're all important.' Princess Margaret

Cut from lustrous Indian sari silk, this outfit was created by the well-known set and costume designer Carl Toms for Princess Margaret to wear at a gold-themed party on the island of Mustique in 1976. Toms assisted Norman Hartnell in the design of Princess Margaret's wedding dress in 1960 but was better known for his set designs and costumes for the theatre and opera. Margaret wore the dress again, without the turban, for a film premiere in London in 1977. It is one of several surviving fancy dress outfits worn by the Princess.

'One hip chick'

Below Sunglasses were a staple of Princess Margaret's wardrobe and she had an extensive collection in varied colours, from the pointed frames she wore at the races in the 1950s (seen here), to the oversized frames she wore from the late 1960s onwards. This photograph was taken in Kingston, Jamaica during the royal tour of the Caribbean in 1955.

Above Princess Margaret's cool, modern image was enhanced with fashionable accessories, such as her elegant cigarette holder and her many pairs of sunglasses. Wearing these oversized Ted Lapidus sunglasses during the 1980s, the Princess exuded an image of relaxed sophistication.

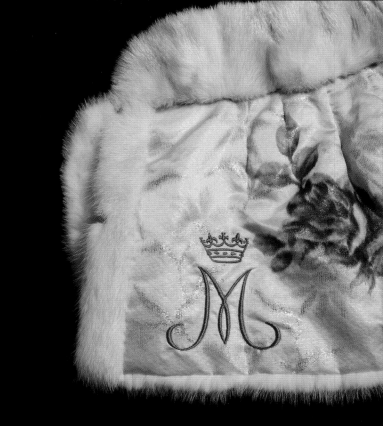

Furs were a glamorous staple of Princess Margaret's wardrobe. In the 1950s she wore fur evening stoles such as this exquisite blonde mink example made by Norman Rogul furs. From the 1960s until later life, she wore mid-length brown fur coats during cold winter evenings.

This stole is lined with floral silk satin printed with grey and pink roses, and features an 'M', surmounted by a crown, embroidered inside.

Diana, Princess of Wales

'She was the most perfect example of a young beautiful and modern woman with her very own style. No fashion victim, but a personality 100 per cent of today.' Karl Lagerfeld

1961–97
Born Lady Diana Spencer, 1 July 1961
Married Charles, Prince of Wales, 29 July 1981
Died 31 August 1997

When her romance with Prince Charles became public in the early 1980s, the young Lady Diana Spencer was thrust into the spotlight. Every outfit she wore was scrutinised by the press. At just 20 years old on her marriage to the Prince of Wales in 1981, she had yet to develop the personal style for which she became famous. Within months of her marriage, however, Diana, Princess of Wales had become a global phenomenon and was developing a wardrobe to match. In the 1980s, her faithful patronage of British designers and much-imitated style was credited with almost single-handedly reviving the flagging British fashion industry, making designers such as Bruce Oldfield and Catherine Walker household names.

Charles and Diana's engagement was announced on 28 February 1981 and much was made in the press of what Diana chose to wear for the occasion. It is said that she had intended to wear a couture garment from Bellville Sassoon but instead bought an 'off the peg' suit from Harrods. The suit was made by London label Cojana and was a bright sapphire blue to complement the Princess's engagement ring. She wore it with a white blouse with blue pattern and an oversized bow at the neck, and flat black pumps. The outfit inspired Diana's first imitators. Lyn Morris, Senior Selector for Marks & Spencer ladies' blouses recalled, 'as soon as Diana did that engagement picture, our fastest selling style was a side-tying Diana blouse'.

Just a week after the engagement was announced, Diana attended her first public engagement as the Prince of Wales's fiancée. For the evening recital at Goldsmiths's Hall, she chose a black taffeta strapless ball gown with a low sweetheart neckline by David and Elizabeth Emanuel. The dress caused a stir amongst the photographers who waited outside to get a picture of Diana, and some fashion journalists said it was too revealing. The public had its first glimpse of the glamorous side of the 19-year-old, who had to make her early fashion faux pas in front of the world's media.

Left Diana, Princess of Wales by Terence Donovan, 1990. *Vogue* fashion editor Anna Harvey commented '[Diana] enjoyed sitting for portraits ... She especially loved Terence Donovan, who made her laugh, and Patrick Demarchelier, who was incredibly flirtatious and not remotely deferential.' For this portrait Diana chose to wear a formal evening dress and bolero jacket by Catherine Walker.

It took some time for the Princess to develop her own style. When she adopted formal dress codes the press criticised her for being 'frumpy'; but her public role and duties meant that the youthful, playful fashion of her contemporaries was equally unsuitable. So the Princess and her mother, Frances Shand Kydd, turned to *Vogue* fashion editor Anna Harvey for advice. Harvey assembled clothes for Diana to choose from and recommended designers who she felt would understand the challenge. Among them was Bruce Oldfield, who developed a lasting friendship with the Princess. He later commented: [We were] 'dressing a young woman who, to an extent, was relying on us to steer her straight, knowing we wouldn't let her down'.

With a group of brilliant designers to work with, Diana's style became more sophisticated and she became the perfect ambassador for British fashion. For daytime events, she chose tailored suits for winter and silk dresses for summer, building up a wardrobe of glamorous evening dresses that flattered her figure and were lauded by press and public. Diana adopted some of the royal customs such as wearing hats and modest hemlines, but dispensed with others which were less suited to her individual style. She rarely wore gloves, preferring more direct contact with the people she met. After some early mistakes she developed a sharp sense of how to dress for public life. In 1985 she explained, 'You'd be amazed what one has to worry about, from the obvious things like the wind – because there's always a gale wherever we go – and the wind is my enemy, there's no doubt about that. And you've got to put your arm up to get some flowers, so you can't have something too revealing, and you can't have hems too short because when you bend over there's six children looking up your skirt.'

Diana was very aware of the power of fashion. The designer John Galliano remarked, 'I always felt she really understood how to use fashion as the silent language and let clothes do the talking for her when she couldn't, the way a movie star in the silent films did.' In 1994, while Jonathan Dimbleby's famous documentary with the Prince of Wales was broadcast, Diana arrived at a gala at London's Serpentine Gallery wearing a strapless, figure-hugging black cocktail dress designed by Christina Stambolian. Images of the confident, radiant Princess were featured on every front page the next day.

The evolution of Diana's style was documented to an unprecedented extent by the British media and paparazzi. The wide availability of images of the Princess both on and off duty, and the speed at which these images were sent around the world made her, in fashion terms, one of the most influential women of the 20th century. Although women around the world imitated her style, Diana was not a fashion leader. Her influence can perhaps best be understood as a 'translator' of fashionable styles. Thousands of women imitated the Princess's latest dress by Bruce Oldfield, her latest hairstyle, her new outfit by Bellville Sassoon. Her power was in making high status and high fashion accessible to a wide audience.

Right On the day her engagement to Prince Charles was announced, Diana wore an 'off the peg' suit from Harrods. The press coverage fixated on the fact that Diana had altered the shop-bought suit herself, taking down the hem to lengthen the skirt: 'Then the girl destined to be the next Queen, got out her needle and thread and stitched it neatly back again.'

Below left Diana's off-duty wardrobe got as much press attention as her dress for public occasions. The Princess soon used these moments as opportunities to promote the charities she supported. At a polo match in Windsor in 1988, the Princess was photographed wearing a fashionable oversized jacket and leather boots with cut-out details, with a sweatshirt displaying the logo of the British Lung Foundation.

Right Like many royal women before her, Diana supported British designers. Here, she is pictured at the Braemar Gathering in 1981 wearing a tartan dress by Caroline Charles and a John Boyd hat.

Below right By the late 1980s, Diana favoured stylish, slim-fitting evening wear such as this Catherine Walker dress and bolero jacket encrusted with pearls and sequins. She wore it to the British Fashion Awards in October 1989 and then on an official visit to Hong Kong. It became known as 'The Elvis Dress' (see page 92).

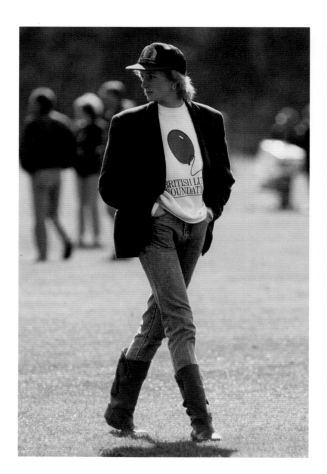

'The most breathtaking
bride in history' *The Daily Mail*

The fairy-tale bride

Below There was unprecedented interest in what Lady Diana Spencer would wear for her wedding to Prince Charles. Details of the dress were under press embargo until the moment she stepped out of the carriage at Westminster Abbey. The dress, by Emanuel, embodied all the romance and drama an adoring public could have hoped for. It had a wide full skirt, bouffant sleeves and long wide train attached at the waist extending 25 feet behind the bride – the longest wedding train in royal history.

Left Diana, Princess of Wales by Lord Lichfield, 1981. In keeping with tradition, Diana's wedding gown was made from British fabrics. The ivory silk taffeta was manufactured using silk from Dorset silk worms and the design included antique lace from Nottingham and Irish Carrickmacross lace from the collection of Queen Mary. There was 'something blue': a small blue bow sewn into the waistband; 'something borrowed': a pair of diamond earrings belonging to the bride's mother; and an 18-carat Welsh-gold horseshoe stitched into the back of the dress for good luck.

'Glamour, glamour, glamour!'

Right The American soap opera 'Dynasty' became hugely popular in the 1980s and the Princess of Wales was known to never miss an episode. The glitzy dresses worn by the lead characters sparked trends for evening wear. These were adopted by the Princess, earning her the nickname 'Dynasty Di'. This dress was made by Bruce Oldfield, who began designing for the Princess in 1981 and created many daytime outfits and bold evening gowns with dramatic details such as high shoulder pads and the revealing deep V-back neckline seen here.

Far right and below This striking midnight blue strapless gown features a theatrical fish-tail skirt with multiple layers of tulle. It was made for the Princess by London designer Murray Arbeid, renowned for his glamorous evening gowns. 'Others do day clothes better', he once said, 'so let them get on with it'. The dress was clearly one of the Princess's favourites. She wore it first in 1986 for a dinner at Claridges and at several other high profile occasions during the 1980s as well as in 1997 for this portrait taken by Lord Snowdon. Arbeid later recalled, 'Those of us who were privileged to make her clothes found ourselves with the perfect client – beautiful – tall – a perfect figure – a world famous real life Princess. What more could a designer possibly ask for?'

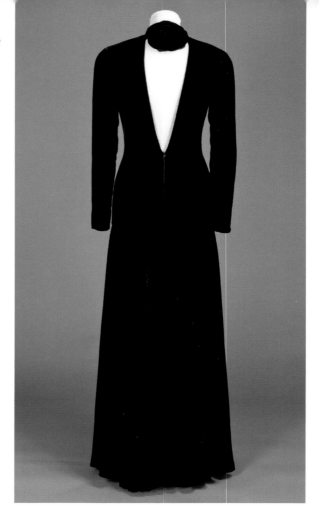

'Less is no longer enough.
Now it's glamour; glamour;
glamour; glamour.'
Bruce Oldfield, *Vogue*, 1981

A working wardrobe

Left Diana, Princess of Wales dressed with considerable flair but she still had a job to do. She embraced some conventions of royal dressing early on, incorporating into her outfits traditional fabrics sourced from the countries she visited during official tours and colours that made reference to her host countries. On the first day of the royal couple's tour of Japan in 1986, the Princess made a bold statement, dressing in a red polka dot dress and red hat from the small high street store Tatters on the Fulham Road. The clear reference to the Japanese flag was a hit with the crowds.

Right The Princess wore this dress by British designer Zandra Rhodes for a state banquet in Kyoto, Japan. Its striking pink colour echoed the cherry blossoms that were in flower at the time of the royal visit. The handkerchief hem and printed lace design gave a petal-like lightness to the dress. Interviewed for *Vogue* in 1981 Rhodes said of 1980s fashions: 'What's very important now is a fantastic feeling for dressing up and looking absolutely wonderful.' Her designs for the Princess of Wales managed to combine the glitz of the decade's look with the romanticism of fairy-tale princesses.

The 1990s

Left In the 1990s Diana adopted a more streamlined and sophisticated look in keeping with changing fashions. Her hair was cut shorter and often worn sleeked back and she favoured pared-down jewellery and make-up. After her official separation from the Prince of Wales in 1992, the Princess started wearing clothes by foreign designers such as Chanel, Valentino, Moschino, Armani and Yves Saint Laurent. Diana no longer had to conform to the royal dress code and wore increasingly body-conscious styles with shorter hemlines, lower necklines and higher heels. The Italian designer Gianni Versace became one of the Princess's favourites. She wore this short black Versace evening dress at the London premiere of the film *Apollo* 13 in 1995. It was simple in its design but caused a stir amongst the press.

Diana's signature look for day was simple, unadorned suits in bright colours with short, straight skirts and elegant shift dresses. For evening she favoured long, glamorous versions of the shift dress style by Versace, Azagury and Catherine Walker worn with high heels by Manolo Blahnik or Jimmy Choo. After 15 years of experimenting, Diana had found a style that suited her. Clothes that were less an expression of her role but that supported the modern, confident woman she had become.

Right Diana, Princess of Wales by Roger Hargreaves, 1995. The Princess was greeted by a crowd of photographers at every public event she attended.

'The Princess's fashion
choices attracted interest
and comment throughout
the world.' Tim Graham

A confident, modern woman

Mario Testino's 1997 photographs of Diana for *Vanity Fair* magazine remain among the most famous portraits of the Princess. This was her last official photo shoot. Diana looked relaxed and radiant; a confident modern woman. Testino remembered: she 'was really divine that day. She looked so happy and fresh and sure of herself'.

The Testino portraits were commissioned to promote the auction of 79 of Diana's dresses by Christie's in New York. The sale, which took place on 25 June 1997, raised over three million dollars for the Princess's favourite charities. Diana selected nine of these dresses for the photo shoot with Testino. All were very simple and slimline (with the exception of one ball gown) and make of tactile fabrics, such as this dark green, double-breasted silk velvet evening dress designed by Catherine Walker in 1992 and worn on a number of private occasions.

'She was really divine that day. She looked so happy and fresh and sure of herself'. Mario Testino

The Duchess of Cambridge at the Garter Service, Windsor Castle, June 2011. She wears a striking headpiece by Rachel Trevor-Morgan and a light grey coat and dress by Katherine Hooker.

Catherine, Duchess of Cambridge

'She always wears the clothes; she doesn't let the clothes take over completely.' Hilary Alexander

1982–
Born Catherine Middleton, 9 January 1982
Married Prince William of Wales, 29 April 2011

Since she entered the spotlight from her first associations with Prince William, every aspect of Catherine Middleton's wardrobe was scrutinised by the press. Now, as Duchess of Cambridge, she has projected a modern royal image, combining formal and casual wear, designer and high street clothes all with an elegant, understated style appropriate to her royal role. Hilary Alexander, Fashion Director for *The Daily Telegraph* remarked, 'she makes fashion accessible and she mixes high street with designer, but also I think most importantly, she always wears the clothes, she doesn't let the clothes take over completely'.

The Duchess of Cambridge has consistently supported British industry by wearing clothes made by British designers. The positive effect of her patronage on the British fashion industry has been immense. When Prince William and Catherine Middleton publically announced their engagement on 16 November 2010, Catherine wore a sapphire blue silk dress by Brazilian born, London-based designer Daniella Issa Helayel, whose eponymous Issa label was established in 2001. The wrap dress was cut low in the neckline, with a hemline just above the knee and long sleeves, appropriate for the time of year. The deep sapphire colour complemented her sapphire and diamond engagement ring. The dress was an instant hit with the public and within 24 hours had sold out in the UK and the US.

Other favoured designers include Jenny Packham, Alice Temperley and Sarah Burton at Alexander McQueen but the Duchess also wears British high street brands including Jaeger, Hobbs, Reiss, L.K. Bennett, Topshop and Whistles. This patronage has been a huge boost for these businesses, as the clothes she wears often sell out within hours of any public appearance. Numerous blogs, websites and mobile apps provide the Duchess's followers with every detail of her outfits and advice on how to copy her style.

The Duchess has adopted some of the long-established conventions of royal dressing in ways that are distinctly modern. For trips abroad, she has worn garments that compliment the host country in some way. During a 2011 royal tour of Canada, the Duchess echoed the colours of the Canadian flag, wearing an entirely red and white outfit, topped with a red hat trimmed with maple leaves (see page 119). The hat was designed by Sylvia Fletcher for the established London hat maker Lock & Co. During a visit to New Zealand in April 2014, she chose to wear a blue tweed suit by a New Zealand designer, Rebecca Taylor. Such considered choices represent a clear continuity with the past. The Queen wore many evening gowns embroidered with national emblems – ferns for New Zealand, cherry blossom for Japan, wattle for Australia – as a compliment to host countries for royal tours abroad during the 1950s and 1960s. Queen Victoria wore tartan fabrics in Scotland and Irish poplin and textiles embroidered with gold shamrocks during a state visit to Ireland in 1849.

Fashion journalists, bloggers, celebrity news websites and magazines have ensured that the Duchess's wardrobe is covered from every angle. Speculation about the price of certain items and the messages they convey has filled thousands of column inches since the royal wedding in 2011. Many journalists have noted the Duchess's tendency to wear the same clothes on multiple occasions. The nautical-style knitted dress by Alexander McQueen that she wore at Wimbledon in 2012 had been worn during the previous year's royal tour of North America. She wore a teal evening gown by Jenny Packham for a charity dinner at the National Portrait Gallery and a second charity event at Kensington Palace. A pair of skinny J Brand jeans, worn multiple times during off-duty moments, a fan-shaped leather clutch bag by Anya Hindmarch and 'those wedges', as the *Daily Mail* called a favourite pair of navy Russell & Bromley cork-soled shoes, convey a dual message of support for the British fashion industry and avoidance of frivolity.

Above After graduating from St Andrews University in 2005 with a BA in Art History, Catherine took up a role as accessories buyer for British high-end, high street clothing chain Jigsaw. During this period she was often seen wearing clothes by the brand and there were early signs of 'the Kate effect' with clothes quickly selling out after she had been seen wearing them.

Right For her public 'debut' as a royal-to-be, Catherine chose a sapphire blue silk dress by London designer Daniella Issa Helayel who remarked: 'We are thrilled with the engagement news and I'm very happy that she has chosen to wear Issa today ... she is a very pretty and lovely girl.'

Left The Duchess of Cambridge chose a stylish cream suit by Alexander McQueen for the christening of Prince George in October, 2013. It was the perfect complement to the Honiton lace christening gown.

Above This Alexander McQueen dress in a fine knit with nautical references in its striped blue trim and sailor-style neckline was worn first by the Duchess during an official visit to Canada and again at Wimbledon in July 2012. It is casual and sporty looking, whilst remaining feminine and elegant. The dress was designed by Sarah Burton, who created Catherine's wedding dress in 2011.

Right For the official state visit of the President of Singapore in October 2014, the Duchess wore a grey Alexander McQueen coat dress and matching hat by Jane Taylor. The coat featured a full skirt and flared sleeves at the wrist.

'Such a fashion moment!'

The wedding of Prince William and Catherine Middleton was hotly anticipated in the press and there was intense speculation over what she might wear. Amazingly, the design and designer remained secret until the moment the bride stepped out of the car at Westminster Abbey. At this point a BBC reporter announced, 'I can tell you now, it has just been confirmed that it is Sarah Burton at Alexander McQueen who designed this dress.' Her fellow reporter gushed, 'I am beside myself. This is such a fashion moment!'

The dress struck a balance between being fashionable and regal. For such a vast and grand setting, the dress had to make a big visual impact. The design shows the influence of Victorian dress in the width of the skirt and bustle-like gathers at the back that were intended to unfold like the petals of a flower extending to form the three-metre-long train, which was carried by the bride's sister, maid of honour, Pippa Middleton. Harold Tillman, Chairman of the British Fashion Council, called the wedding a victory for British fashion. Of the dress, he said, 'I think it's just perfection.'

Although traditional in design, the dress was constructed of a relatively modern fabric: heavy silk gazar and covered with lace appliqué work. The traditional Cluny and Leavers lace was assembled by the Royal School of Needlework who incorporated the national symbols of roses, thistles, shamrocks and daffodils. Work on the lace was carried out at their studios at Hampton Court Palace by embroiderers aged from 19 to 70. In order to keep the lace and thread pristine, their needles were renewed every three hours and there was a strict regime of hand washing every 30 minutes. Even the embroiderers working on the lace did not know who had designed the dress.

It was a precious, magical time that I'll always treasure, and I feel like she gave me a gift in many ways. I feel incredibly privileged.'

Sarah Burton on designing the Duchess of Cambridge's wedding dress

Trusted designers

Right Like most women in the public eye, and many royal women before her, the Duchess of Cambridge has a handful of trusted designers to whom she turns for the clothing she wears for major public events. Many of the Duchess's most memorable appearances have featured dresses designed by Jenny Packham. At her first official royal engagement following the wedding, the Duchess wore a champagne-coloured evening dress that evoked old-style Hollywood glamour with its heavily embellished fabric and body skimming cut. Jenny Packham is well-known for luxurious embellishment, which makes her designs a popular choice for the red carpet.

Above left The year after their marriage, the Duke and Duchess of Cambridge attended several public engagements surrounding the 2012 London Olympics. At a celebration for British athletes involved in the games, the Duchess wore this teal coloured Jenny Packham evening dress with button-up back in lace and Swarovski crystals. Packham has also designed day dresses for the Duchess, including the dress she wore as she left the hospital with the newborn Prince George.

Left The Duchess of Cambridge has commissioned many garments from Alexander McQueen since the royal wedding in 2011. On the royal tour of South Asia in 2012, a dinner with the Malaysian Head of State required a formal gown appropriate for the occasion. The Duchess chose an Alexander McQueen dress of silk tulle, with gold appliquéd hibiscus flowers, the national flower of Malaysia. This reference to the host country echoed a long tradition of diplomatic dressing within the royal family.

The 'Kate effect'

Below left The Duchess of Cambridge has been widely praised for the economy and accessibility of her clothing choices. She has frequently worn dresses by UK high street label Reiss. Their white silk 'Nanette' dress sold out overnight after the Duchess wore it for the official engagement portrait taken by Mario Testino in 2010. At one stage Reiss was selling one per minute online. Similarly, the royal blue Issa dress worn by the Duchess when the engagement was announced, sold out in less than 24 hours and stocks of the copycat version by Tesco were gone within an hour of being released.

Below right The Duchess chose another Reiss dress to meet the President and First Lady of the United States at Buckingham Palace during their visit to London in May 2011. The camel-coloured 'Shola' dress was in such high demand after this appearance that the store's website crashed. The brand's founder, David Reiss said, 'We're really proud that Kate is a Reiss customer ... and that she has chosen one of our dresses for such an important occasion ... she has the eyes of the world on her and is an incredible ambassador.'

Right The Duchess of Cambridge in Canada during the 2011 royal tour, wearing the 'Nanette' Reiss dress, this time with a red maple leaf hat by Lock & Co. The Duchess is well-known for wearing outfits more than once, and much has been made of her economical approach to dressing. Efforts to economise are not unusual in royal dressing. The Queen often wears her dresses on more than one occasion and has been known to recycle items from her wardrobe from past decades.

'There is no one else who has an effect like her. It has really brought British fashion to the forefront again ... She's been brilliant for British fashion and great for the whole economy.' Alice Temperley

Acknowledgements

Illustrations

Abbreviations:
b= bottom, c = centre, l = left, r = right, t = top

Bridgeman Images: pages 10l (Royal Collection Trust © Her Majesty Queen Elizabeth II, 2015), 10r Private Collection); Corbis: pages 52 (©Hulton-Deutsch Collection), 53t (© The Francis Frith Collection), 110 (Paul Hadfield/Splash News); Photograph Terence Donovan © Terence Donovan Archive: page 92; Getty Images: pages 7 (Topical Press Agency), 8l (Keystone), 8r (Anwar Hussein), 12 (Lichfield), 13t (WPA Pool), 14 (David Levenson), 15t (Lichfield), 16l (Toronto Star Archives), 16r (Samir Hussein), 17 (Keystone), 18 (IWM), 19 (Max Mumby/Indigo), 20 (Chris Ware), 21 (Tim Graham), 22 (Hulton Archive), 28b (Hulton Archive), 34 (W&D Downey), 36 (Popperfoto), 38 (Fox Photos), 40 (W&D Downey), 41r (Heritage Images), 45 (Print Collector), 67l and 67r (Popperfoto), 68 (Samir Hussein), 75r (Keystone-France), 78r (Chris Jackson), 79 (Chris Jackson), 82t (Hulton Archive), 82bl (Hulton Archive), 86 (Central Press), 90b (Popperfoto), 95 (Tim Graham), 96l (Tim Graham), 97 (Anwar Hussein/Wire Image), 98 (Lichfield), 102 (Tim Graham), 104 (Tim Graham), front cover and 108 (WPA Pool), 111 (Mark Cuthbert), 112 (WPA Pool), 113l (George Pimentel), 114 (WPA Pool), 115 (Chris Jackson), 116t (Samir Hussein), 116b (Pool), 117 (Samir Hussein), 118r (Toby Melville/AFP), 119 (Chris Jackson); Stephen Hayward: page 107; © Historic Royal Palaces. Photograph: Robin Forster/www.images.hrp.org.uk: pages 26, 31, 32l, 33, 100t, 103; Murray Arbeid Dress, copyright collector/Designer Pat Kerr (Mrs John Tigrett): page 100b (detail); © Museum of London: page 83r; © National Portrait Gallery, London: pages 4, 25, 27, 30, 50, 51 (© Estate of Paul Tanqueray), 55, 56, 82br (© William Hustler and Georgina Hustler), 105 (© Roger Hargreaves); Press Association Images: page 58l (Len Putnam/AP); Prudence Cuming Associates © Her Majesty Queen Elizabeth II, 2001: page 35; © RMN: page 58r (Grand Palais); © Rex Shutterstock: pages 77t (Ronald Fortune/Daily Mail), 113r; Royal Collection Trust/All Rights Reserved: pages 54t, 57, 59, 70, 72; Royal Collection Trust © Her Majesty Queen Elizabeth II, 2015: pages 5, 6, 13b, 28t, 29, 32r, 41l, 42, 43, 44, 46, 47, 53b, 54b, 62b, 63, 69, 71, 74, 75l, 76, 77b, 78l; Royal Collection Trust/© Viscount Linley and Lady Sarah Chatto: pages 2, 3, 15b, 83l, 85, 88, 89l and back cover, 89r, 90t, 91; The Cecil Beaton Studio Archive at Sotheby's: page 61; Mario Testino/art partner licensing: pages 106, 118l; © Topfoto: pages 84 (AP), 99 (Woodmansterne); Photograph by Snowdon/Trunk Archive: page 101; © Victoria & Albert Museum, London: pages 9, 11, 39 (Lafayette), 48, 60, 62t, 64, 66, 73, 80, 87 (Cecil Beaton), 96r.

Published by Historic Royal Palaces
Hampton Court Palace, Surrey, KT8 9AU.

© Historic Royal Palaces, 2015

ISBN 978-1-873993-36-1

Written by Deirdre Murphy and Cassie Davies-Strodder
Edited by Clare Murphy
Picture research by Clare Murphy and Annie Heron
Designed by Level Partnership
Printed by BKT

Front cover: The Duchess of Cambridge at the Garter Service, June 2011, wearing a headpiece by Rachel Trevor-Morgan (see page 108). Page 2 and back cover: Detail of a turban worn by Princess Margaret in 1976 (see page 89).

Historic Royal Palaces is a registered charity (no. 1068852)
www.hrp.org.uk

 Find us on Facebook: **Historic Royal Palaces**

 Follow us on Twitter: **@HRP_palaces**

 Watch us on YouTube:
youtube.com/HistoricRoyalPalaces

Historic Royal Palaces is the charity that looks after:

Tower of London
Hampton Court Palace
Banqueting House
Kensington Palace
Kew Palace
Hillsborough Castle

We help everyone explore the story of how monarchs and people have shaped society, in some of the greatest palaces ever built.

We raise all our own funds and depend on the support of our visitors, members, donors, sponsors and volunteers.